Illustrated Fluteplaying
2nd (revised) edition

Robin Soldan and Jeanie Mellersh

Acknowledgements

I should like to thank Dr David Baker, M. Phil., D.M., F.F.A.R.C.S. for his expert advice on the mechanisms of breathing; my many colleagues in the Hampshire County Music Service who suggested I should write a book and gave me enthusiastic support during this book's inception; the flute players and teachers too numerous to mention individually who have given me endless ideas through their playing and teaching; the many hundreds of pupils that I have enjoyed teaching over the past thirty years, and from whom I have learnt so much; and, of course, my co-author Jeanie Mellersh.

Robin Soldan

I should like to thank Linda Banks for her help in book design; Bob McFall for editing; the many fluteplayers, especially James Galway, whom I have drawn and to whom I have talked about their playing techniques; Nick, my husband, for the index; all the players who have posed for the pictures, particularly Sarah Parry who helped to get the book started; and, of course, my co-author Robin Soldan.

Jeanie Mellersh

Illustrated Fluteplaying

Text ©   Robin Soldan   1986, 1993
Illustrations ©   Jeanie Mellersh   1986, 1993

Printed in the United Kingdom. All rights reserved. No part of this book may be used or reproduced in any manner whatsoever without written permission, except in the case of brief quotations embodied in critical articles and reviews.

London Minstead Publications, Hilltop Farmhouse,
Minstead, Hampshire, SO43 7FT, England.

Contents

- Page 1. Getting Started
- 5. Starting to Blow
- 16. Holding the Flute
- 20. Posture
- 26. Hand Positions
- 34. Shoulders & Elbows
- 36. Tonguing
- 42. Breathing
- 54. Dynamics & Tuning
- 62. Vibrato
- 66. Blowing Problems
- 77. Index

Introduction

This book is intended for flute players of all ages and standards who want a clear guide to the basics of tone and technique, and who are keen to improve their sound. It can be used as a companion to good flute lessons and methods, helping to prevent those all too common "bad habits" of blowing, breathing and technique which are often very difficult to eradicate later on.

The most important message to any wind player, but perhaps particularly to flute players, is that 95% of the sound, resonance, expression, nuances and general technique come from the player—his or her **entire body** is used in truly successful playing. The flute itself is merely an additional aid to musicianship, with its own very distinct character, to be mastered in a particular way. Unless this fact is clearly appreciated, no amount of experimenting with more and more expensive flutes and headjoints will make the slightest difference to a player's sound. The subtle difference between instruments will begin to become apparent once all the physical controls of playing from the whole body are correct.

The text is copiously illustrated with detailed drawings, making each point in the simplest and clearest way. All basic topics are covered, including tone production, breathing, tonguing, posture, hand positions, vibrato, playing in tune, dynamics etc, and a section on "blowing problems" deals with some of the most frequent causes of poor tone quality. The drawings are designed so that young children can grasp the point immediately, without having to read a lot of text, but we hope that the verbal information will prove useful to all students, and to woodwind teachers who teach the flute although it may not be their main instrument.

The ideas in this book are generally shared by most flute teachers today, but there will probably be some areas of disagreement over details. A description of the subtleties involved in playing the flute can never replace the experience of listening to and learning from a first class performer, and of course no two performers play with exactly the same sound and expression; it would, after all, be dull if they did, and if there was only one "correct way" of playing any instrument. This book represents one well tried pathway towards achieving control over the instrument, so that we can eventually forget about the technical details and concentrate on the much more enjoyable business of making good music.

Getting Started

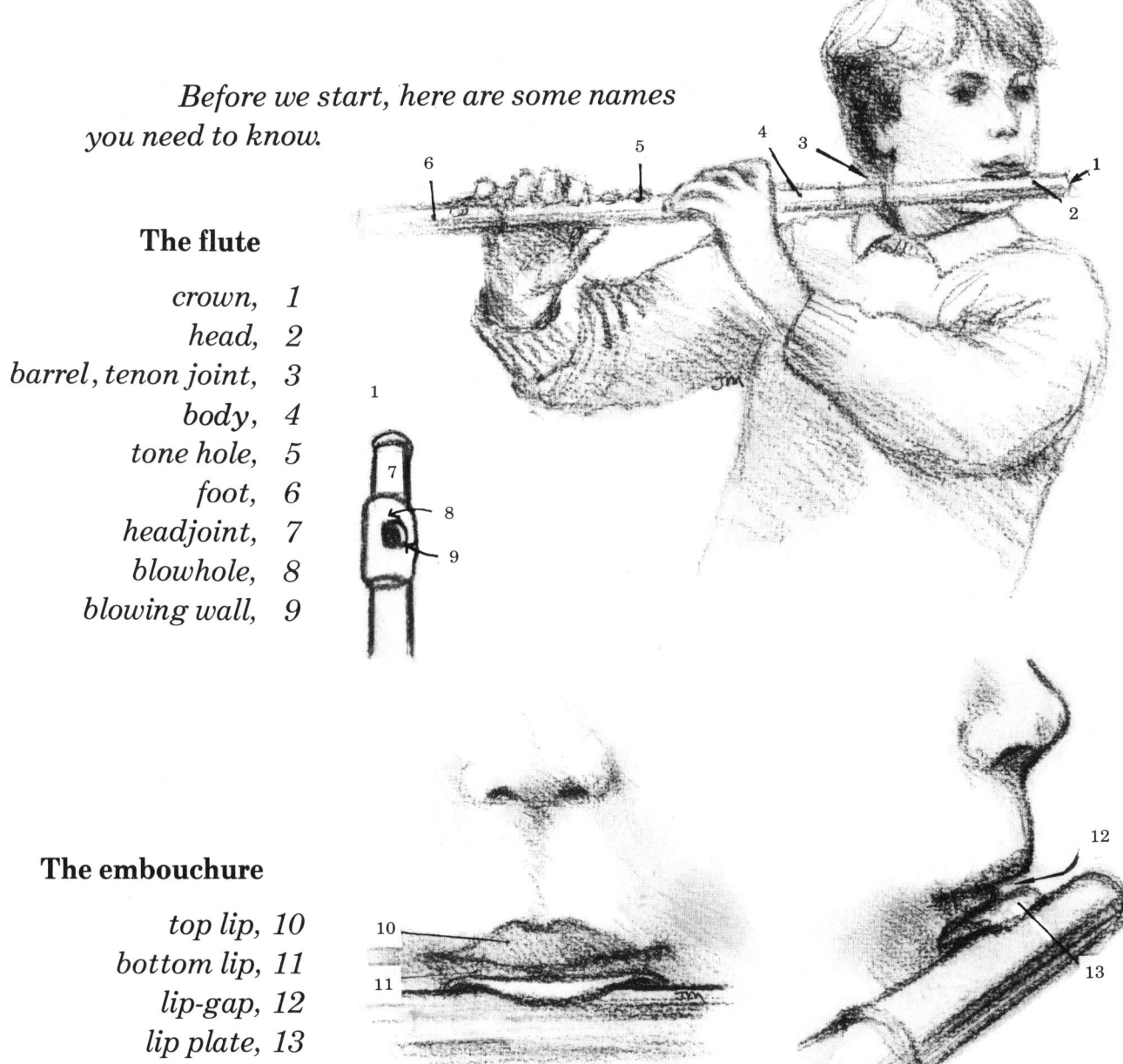

Before we start, here are some names you need to know.

The flute

crown, 1
head, 2
barrel, tenon joint, 3
body, 4
tone hole, 5
foot, 6
headjoint, 7
blowhole, 8
blowing wall, 9

The embouchure

top lip, 10
bottom lip, 11
lip-gap, 12
lip plate, 13

Over the page you will learn how to assemble the flute.

Illustrated Fluteplaying

1. Putting the headjoint on

First make sure the surfaces of the joint are clean and free from grease — wipe any dirt or grease off with a cloth.

Grip the headjoint with your left hand and hold the body with your right hand round the barrel, not the keys. Use a twisting action, don't waggle or force it on.
Push it right home as far as it will go. (You may need to pull out slightly for tuning — this is explained later.)

Don't grip the lip-plate — it could come off or bend out of shape.

2. Lining up the headjoint

*Get into the habit of lining up every time you put the flute together, in exactly the same position to suit **you**; you can only find the perfect position for your best sound after some experience. So at first line up the middle of the blow-hole with the middle of the first **large** hole on top of the body — **not** with the small hole.*

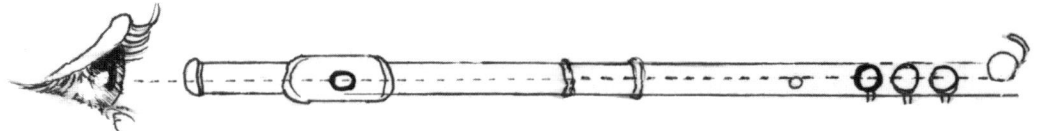

3. Putting the foot-joint on

Hold the body in the left hand, avoiding the keys, by the barrel, and twist the foot-joint on, holding it firmly round the long rod with thumb of the right hand.

Line up the long rod with the middle of the last key in the body.

*Remember to **twist** and **push** — never use a waggling movement. A close air-tight fit is essential — not only will a loose fit mean weak notes, but if the foot-joint works loose and drops off it could be badly damaged, needing expensive repairs.*

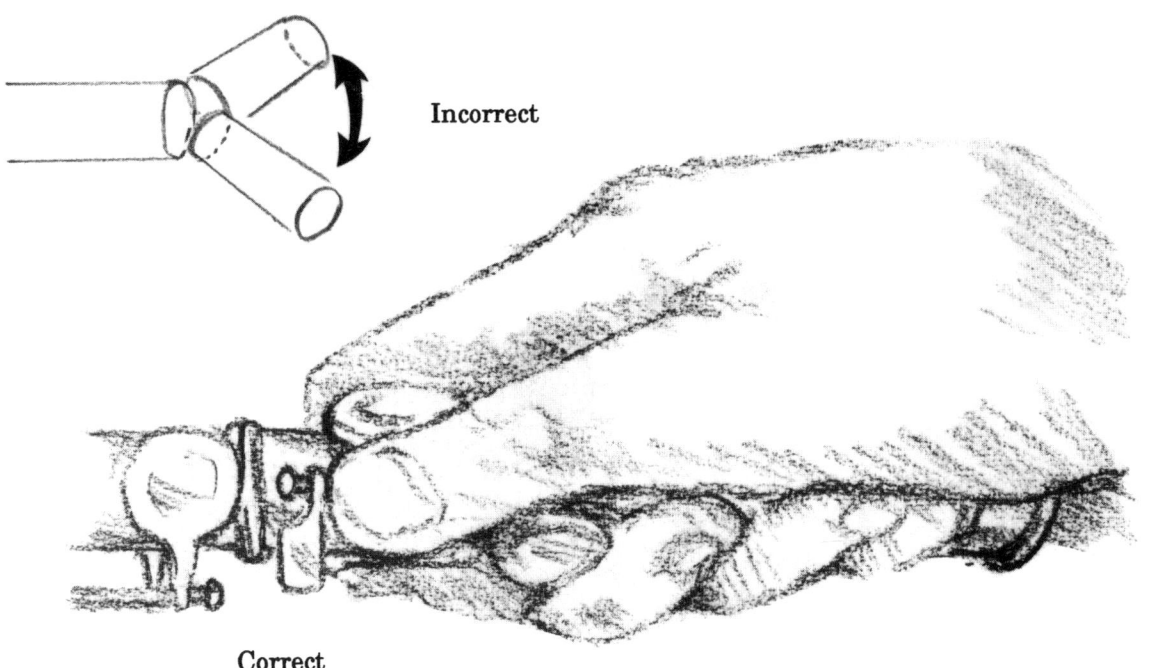

Incorrect

Correct

4 *Illustrated Fluteplaying*

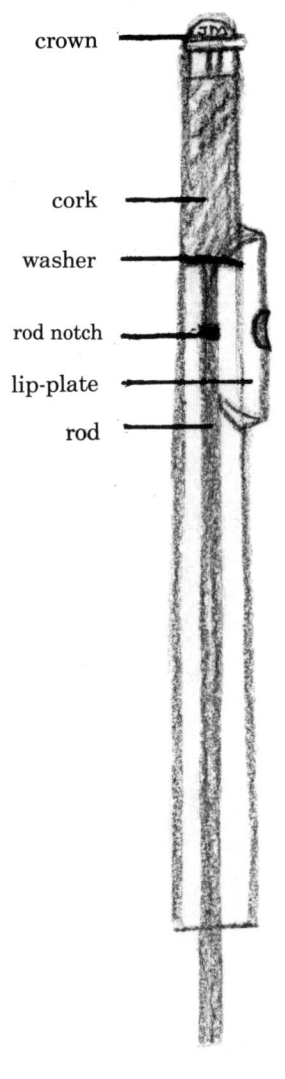

crown
cork
washer
rod notch
lip-plate
rod

Cleaning the flute

*Keep the joints clean, and **never** grease the metal — grease attracts dust and dirt, which act as abrasives.*

Keep the outside clean with a soft cloth, and occasionally polish with a cloth impregnated with silver polish, not with liquid polish that might clog up the mechanism.

Always dry the inside of the flute after use to prevent moisture from making the pads spongy or sticky. Use a cleaning-rod, not a mop (which has fibres that come off).

Thread a piece of silk or cotton material through the eye of the rod and pass it up the headjoint and through the separated sections of the flute before replacing the flute in its case.

The cleaning-rod should have a notch at one end for checking the cork position — a wrong cork position affects tone and tuning quite drastically. Place the rod inside the headjoint till it touches the cork — the notch should appear half-way along the blow-hole.

The cork is out of sight between the crown and the lip-plate. It has a metal washer attached at both ends.

Starting to Blow

Lip Work

There are three stages to this exercise. Sit facing your mirror:

1. *Finger is substituted for flute. Press index finger firmly against soft underside of bottom lip.*
*Keep finger **STRAIGHT**.*

2. *Feel that your bottom lip is straight along the length of your finger, drooping over it, quite floppy, and then very slightly stretch your bottom lip at each end, as in saying "**EE**", firming it slightly.*

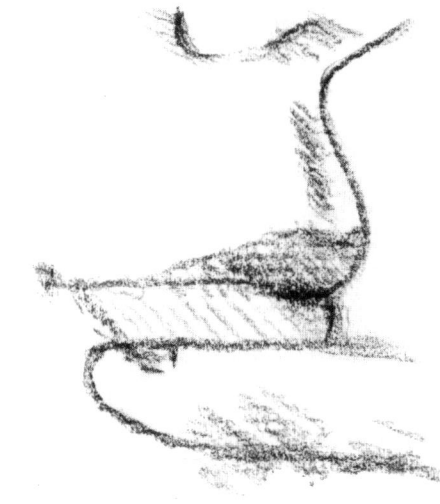

3. *The muscle in the top lip needs to be firm and responsive. By using this muscle learn to push your top lip down onto your bottom lip and blow quite hard. Push top lip down until the hole you are blowing through is very small and the air makes a hissing sound, like squeezing a balloon neck or stopping a bicycle-pump end with your thumb.*

*Next, repeat this exercise on the **tube** of the headjoint, beside the lip-plate.*

Illustrated Fluteplaying

The Pout

Watch a young child pout just before tears flow; the chin comes forward and up, and the inside of the bottom lip shows.

*The **centre** of the bottom lip should remain in a pout, although the ends are firm.*

Rabbit Exercise

You have to develop a lot of strength in the muscles controlling the top lip so plenty of rabbit exercises will help.

With your headjoint in place on lower lip move top lip up and down like a rabbit does when eating. Blow and feel the air being squeezed into a narrow jet as you bring your top lip firmly down each time you blow.

After a lot of exercises you may feel the muscles round your embouchure beginning to tingle, and perhaps even bulge slightly as they strengthen.

Starting to Blow 7

Lip Press-Ups

Make sure the air jet is more narrow than the blowhole. If you have difficulty making a really narrow air-jet because your top-lip seems too floppy or too short to stretch right down onto your bottom lip, **lip press-ups** *may help!*

Sitting on a chair with your elbows on the table, put both index fingers under top lip, and push head hard down onto fingers, keeping your top lip completely firm.

Drop your head down, press head up, alternately firming and relaxing top lip.

This exercise must be repeated hundreds of times to have any real effect, but it should prove helpful to people with particular blowing problems (see pages 66 to 72, 73).

Ideally you should develop a well-controlled lip-gap capable of being very small (almost invisible). Beginners take time to do this.

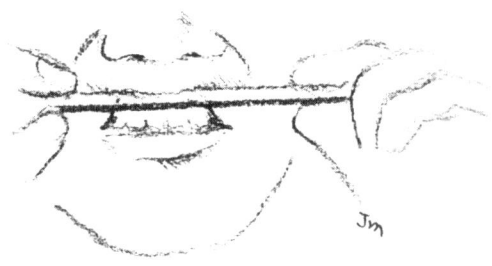

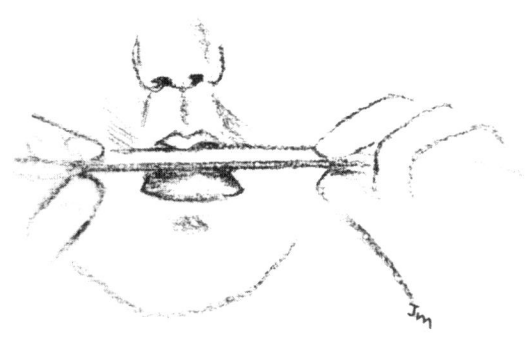

8 ***Illustrated Fluteplaying***

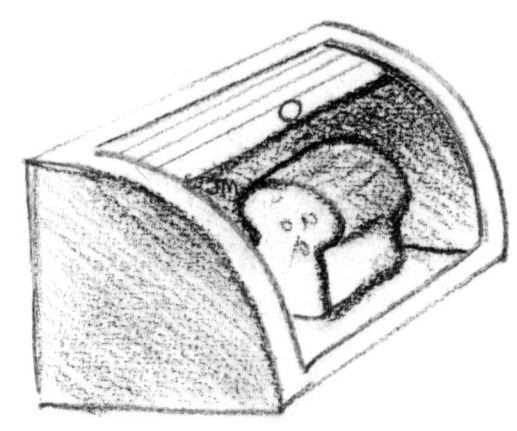

Headjoint Work

Take the headjoint alone. Place bottom lip along the lip-plate as you did on your finger, and on the tube, so that one-third of the blow-hole is covered by your bottom lip.

Shaded part shows area covered by bottom lip.

*Be very careful not to put the lip-plate **too low** on your bottom lip — it should be as high as possible, but still allow just enough lip to partially cover the hole.*

The breadbin exercise.

*Try to get into the habit of pushing your top lip forward and down, so that when you blow a note, your top lip is further forward than your bottom lip. If you find this difficult, you can do exercises to help: make your top lip **stretch** so that it touches the far side of the blow-hole.*

Top lip moves forward and down like the lid of a roll-top breadbin.

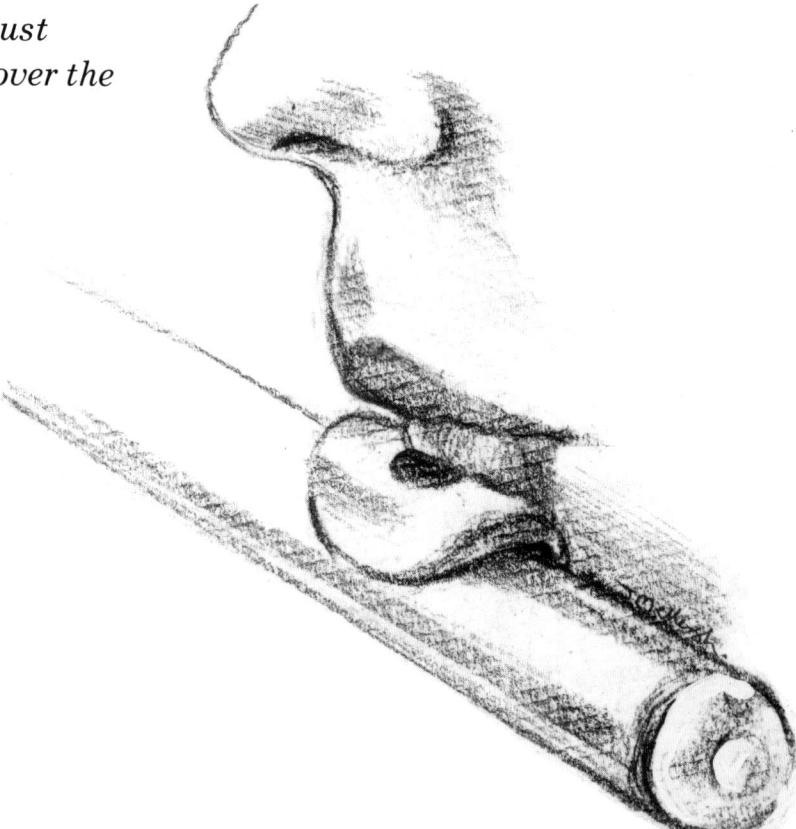

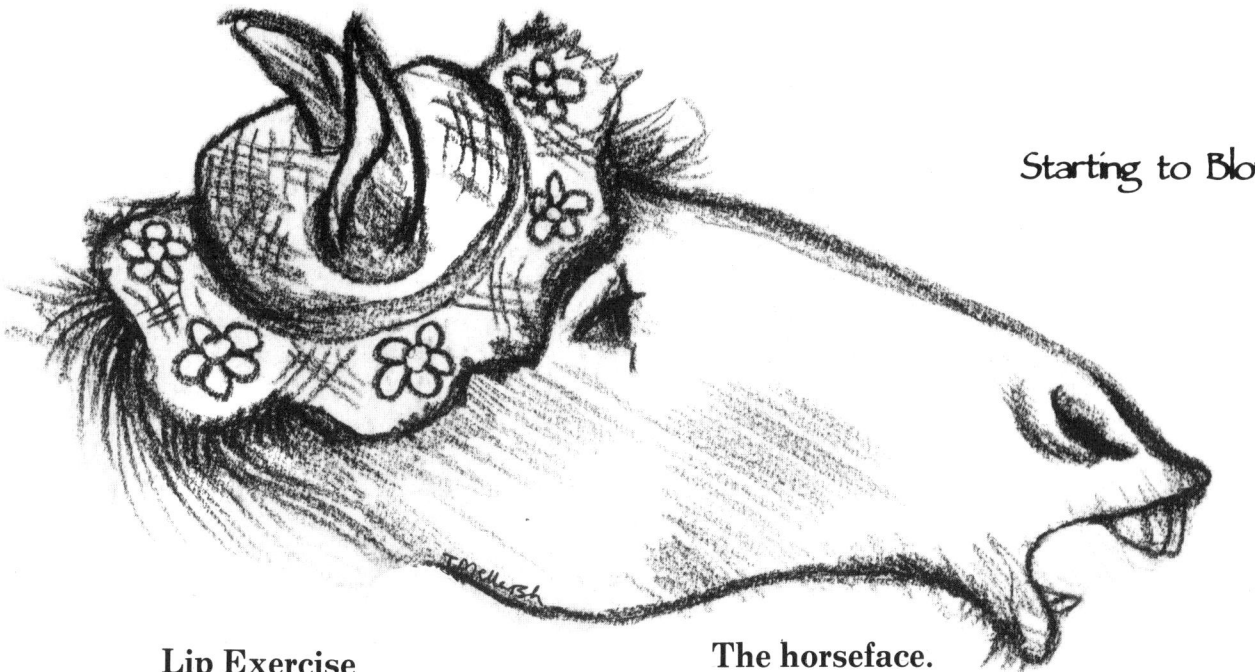

Starting to Blow 9

Lip Exercise

*Facing a mirror, practise moving your top lip right up and down onto your bottom lip **without moving bottom lip!***

Lift your top lip well above teeth.
Don't contort the rest of your face.
Feel your nostrils being stretched downwards, together with your whole top-lip area.
Press down firmly.

The horseface.

*Make your face **long** and **horse-like** as you push down.*

Try not to stretch your bottom lip into a curve away from your finger, as this may spoil the shape of the lip-gap. Stretch the corners out, "EE", but don't pull them back towards your ears like a smile.

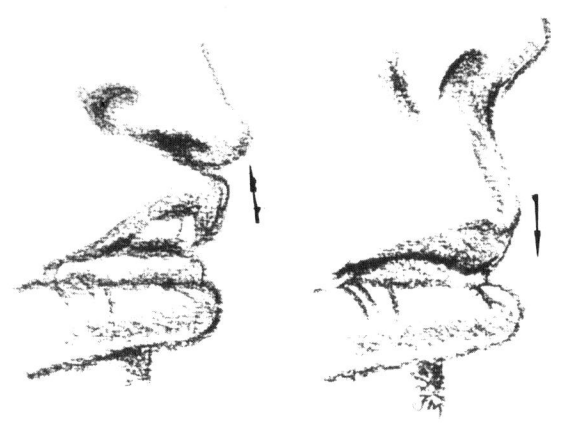
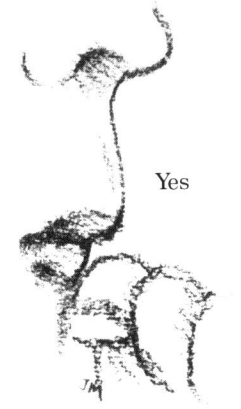
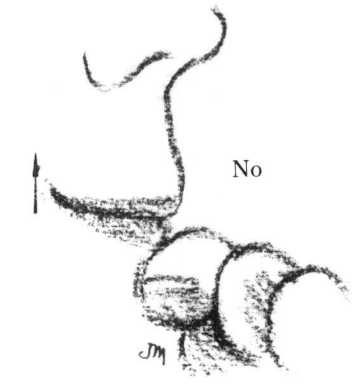

*The muscles which **pull** the top lip down are the **scowling** muscles, BELOW the lower lip: these must get strong.*

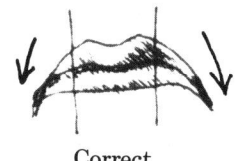

Correct

Incorrect

Illustrated Fluteplaying

Jaw Movements

*The jaw is used a lot for making small adjustments to tone, tuning and dynamics. Practise pushing the jaw backwards and forwards against the pressure of your finger with your mouth open; avoid up and down movements (as in eating) — use only small **horizontal** movements.*

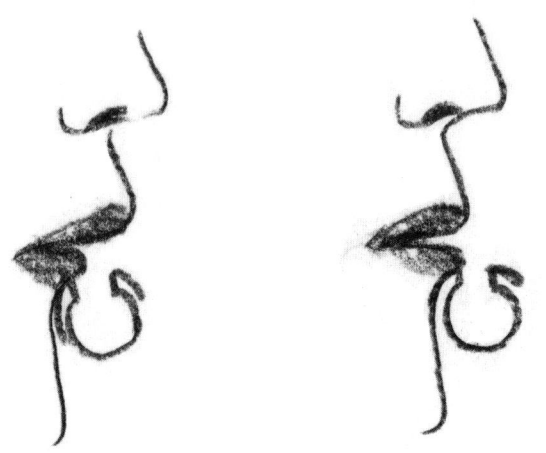

Feel the hinge or your jawbone moving when you place your fingers about an inch below your ears.

*With the headjoint, feel a constant pressure between your bottom lip and the lip-plate, squeezing the headjoint **firmly** against the jaw pushing against your gums.*

 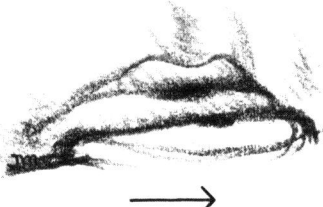

Starting to Blow 11

Rolling The Headjoint In or Out

To find the position of the headjoint on your lip that produces the best sound, experiment by rolling the headjoint in and out as you blow until you make a strong, clear sound.
The best sound will be when about one-third of the blow-hole is covered.

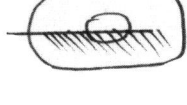
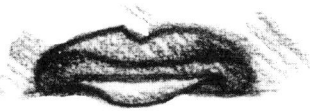
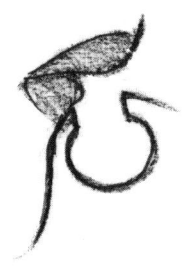
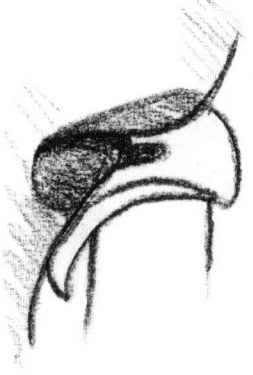

Correct

*Rolling it in too much causes too much blow-hole to be covered, and **the sound is flat and stifled.***

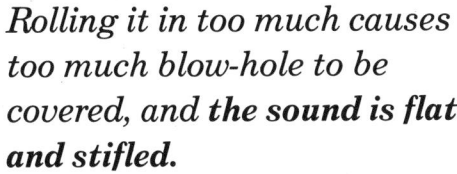

Incorrect

*Rolling it out too much uncovers all the blow-hole and the sound is **weak, woolly and sharp.***

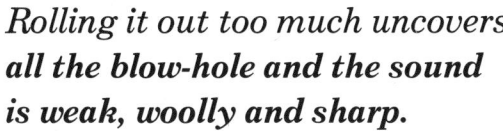
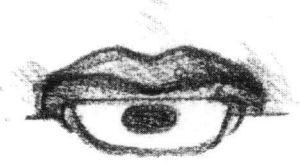

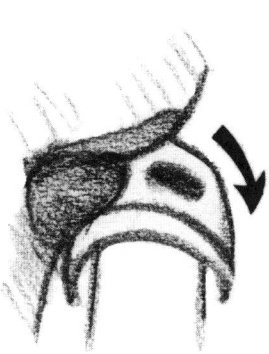

Incorrect

Illustrated Fluteplaying

Experiments with headjoint sounds.

← *Practise blocking the end of the headjoint with your hand as you play a clear note, then play with the end open. You may feel a slight muscle change in your embouchure between the two notes.*

Also try making high and low → notes by sliding a finger in and out of the headjoint as you blow, and allowing your embouchure to get used to the tiny adjustments necessary on each note.

Then try to blow the higher notes obtainable on the headjoint — the harmonics — which need a lot more puff.

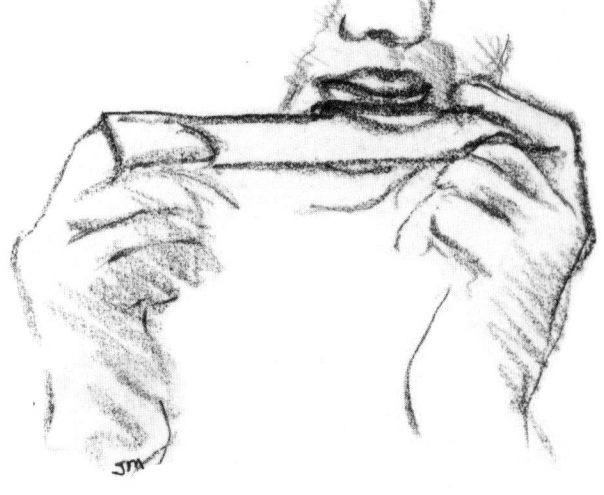

Aim to produce a strong well- → focused sound on the headjoint every time you pick it up. Now put the whole flute together and blow a note without pressing any keys.

Starting to Blow 13

Here are some good embouchures.

When a player makes a good sound, it is often difficult to see the blow-hole and the lip-gap.

Top lip forward and down

Bottom lip straight and floppy **making contact all along the lip-plate.**

14 *Illustrated Fluteplaying*

The Three Controls

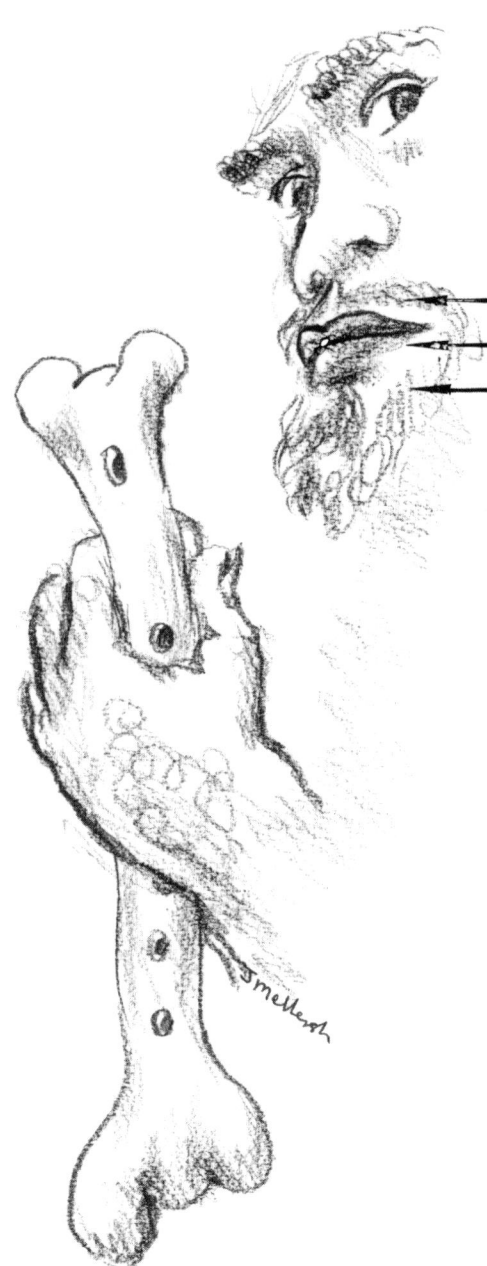

The lip and jaw movements described in the previous pages can be summed up as three basic "controls" for the embouchure:

juggle with the three controls

*1. **Top lip**
2. **Bottom lip**
3. **Jaw***

When you play, you must be able to move these either altogether or separately and independently.

Of course no two people have the same shaped face and lips, so you have to experiment with the three controls to obtain the best result. As a general rule, the controls are used so that:

*1. Top lip is pushing forward and down.
2. Bottom lip is straight, pouting slightly over hole.
3. Jaw is pushing forward against the lip-plate.*

When you watch a good player you may not notice any movement of the embouchure at all, but most players are in fact making small adjustments to the three controls to maintain an even and focused sound. These adjustments are extremely delicate and precise.

Starting to Blow   15

The Lip Gap

The shape of the lip-gap is extremely important for producing the best sound. Experienced players are able to make fine adjustments to the three controls to let them maintain exactly the correct size and shape of the lip-gap for each note. A fairly deep, funnel-shaped gap is the most effective, with the narrowest part on the outside of the lips, and a slight increase in the dimensions of the gap towards the inside: this tapering shape enables the air-jet to emerge at just the right speed and angle.

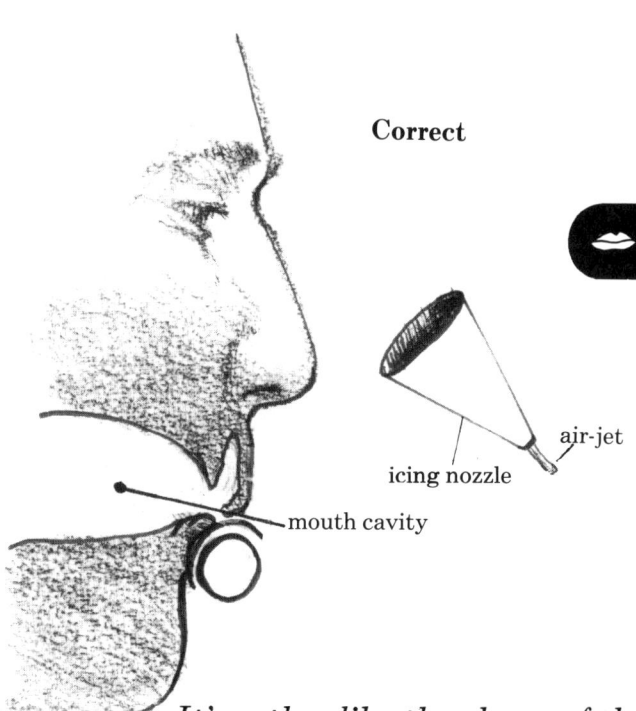

Correct

It's rather like the shape of the nozzle used in cake icing.

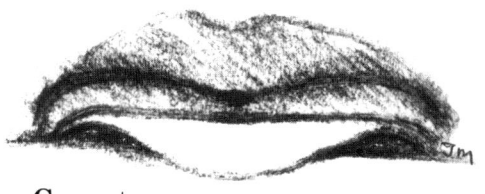

Correct   Lip gap very small and hardly visible

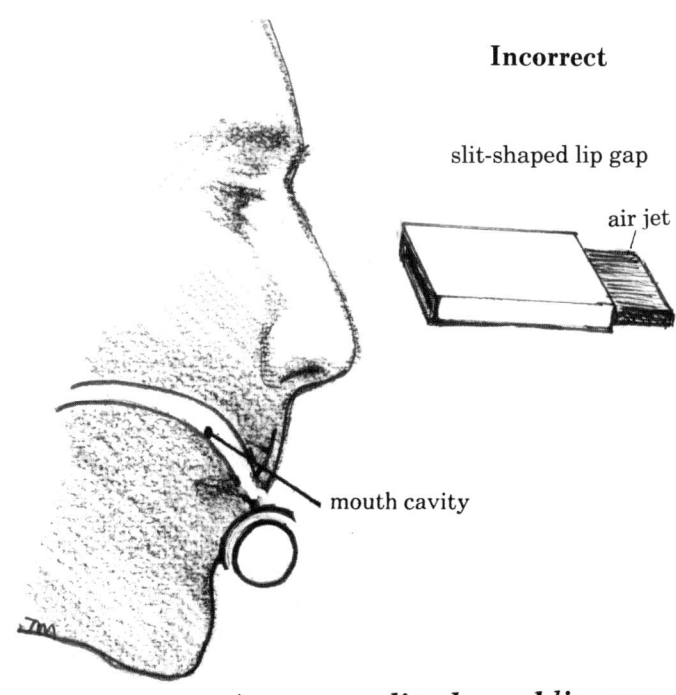

Incorrect

*A narrow **slit-shaped** lip-gap tends to produce a weaker, unfocused sound.*

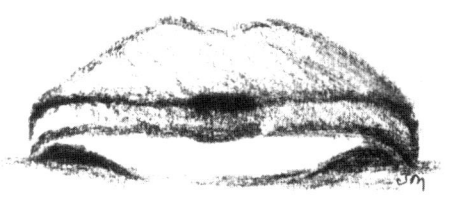

Incorrect   Lip-gap too large

Holding the Flute

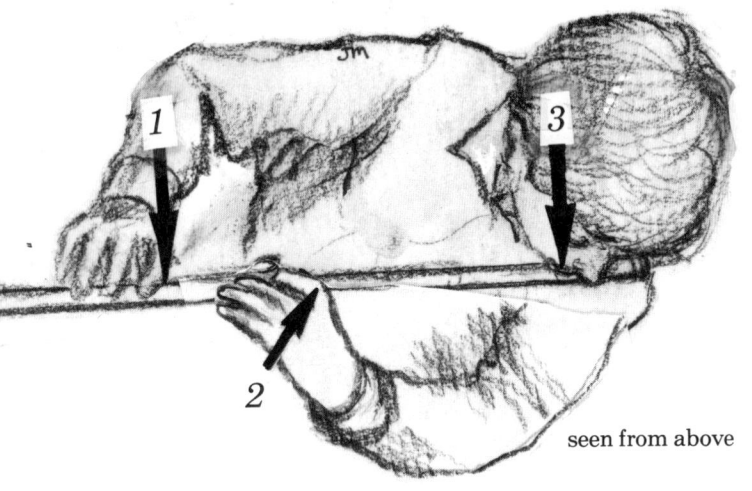

seen from above

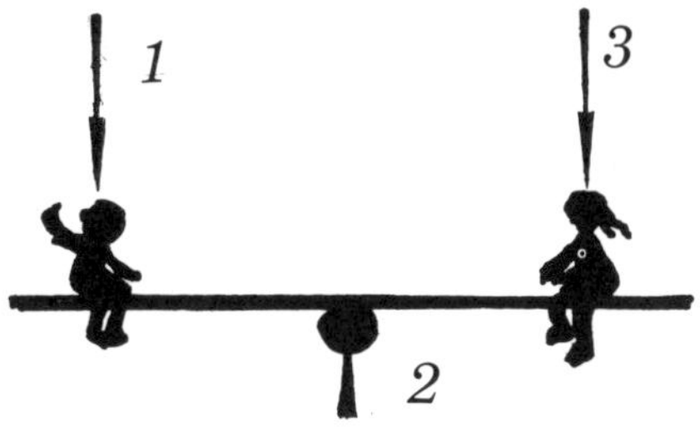

The Pressure Points

To hold the flute at the correct angles, and to prevent it from wobbling about while playing (which would ruin any chance of controlling the sound), we need to use the three pressure points (shown in the picture by arrows).

1. Right thumb

2. Left-hand index finger

3. Jaws and gums

*Push the flute **firmly** towards you with the fleshy part of the first joint of the **left index finger:***

You will find that your finger goes a bit red and gets flattened by the pressure.

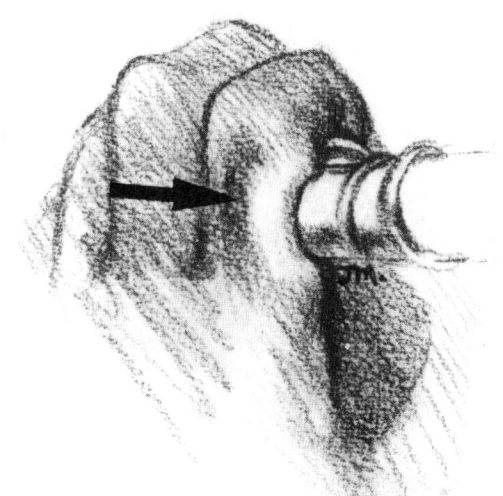

think of the pressures like a see-saw

Holding the Flute 17

The jaw keeps a forward pressure against the push of the index finger, and the flesh below your bottom lip squashes against your gums (which may ache a bit after playing).

The right thumb is placed on the flute so that it can push away from your right shoulder, against the pressure of the left index finger. After a lot of playing the thumb may get a bit sore as well, and the skin might become hardened.

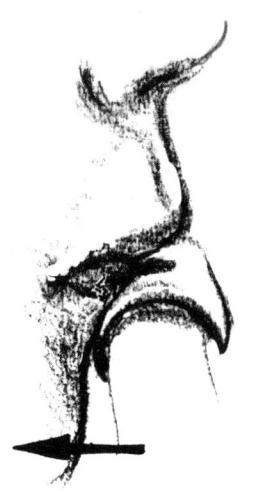

*Using these pressure points correctly **allows** you to move all the playing fingers easily and fluently without the flute feeling insecure — there should never be even the **slightest** unintentional wobble of the flute on your lips! The balanced pressure of jaw against index finger makes it possible to control the delicate lip and jaw movements needed for fine tuning and focusing of the sound.*

Furthermore, a strong pressure-hold will improve your sound — the flute will feel PART of you: when everything is going right, you'll get a real sense of being part of the sound, creating it with your whole body.

With some fingerings, you might feel that the flute is feeling insecure unless the pressure-points are being used for example C-D-E-D-C-D-E-D

18 *Illustrated Fluteplaying*

Getting the Angles Right.

The best, most focused sound is more easily obtained when all the holding angles are correct, so that there is no imbalance in the muscles of the embouchure, arms or body, and the blowing can be finely controlled without any strain.

1. *Flute and body angle.*

As you can see on page 34, the flute should be pushed away from the right shoulder, the head turned towards the left, with the trunk slightly pivoted, again towards the left, at the waist.

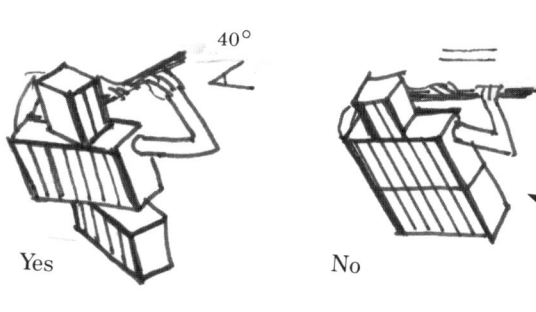

Yes   No

*There is an angle of about 40° between the **line of the shoulders** and the **line of the flute**.*

2. *Flute and head angle.*

Most players hold the flute at an angle dipping slightly downwards rather than horizontal, parallel to the floor:

This dipping angle stops the arms from getting tired, and keeps the shoulders low and relaxed (best for good breathing).

With the flute up, horizontal, you may find your arms and shoulders begin to ache, tensions develop, breathing is less effective, so your tone suffers.

*If the flute is held **parallel** to the shoulders, head held to the front, neck and shoulder aches will develop, and the tone will suffer because breathing is affected (see page 51).*

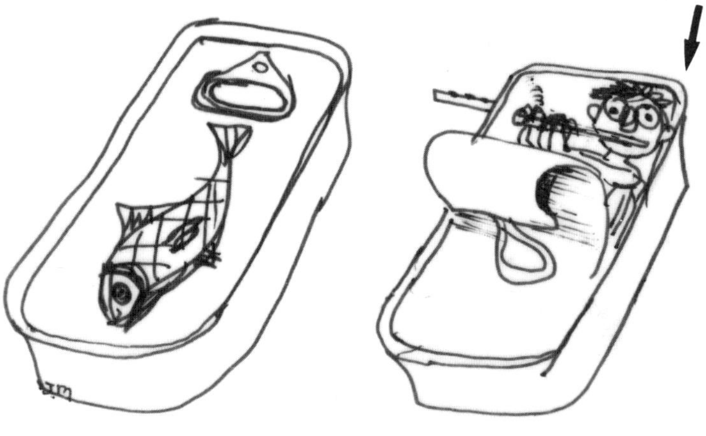

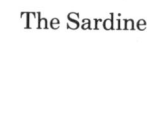

The Sardine

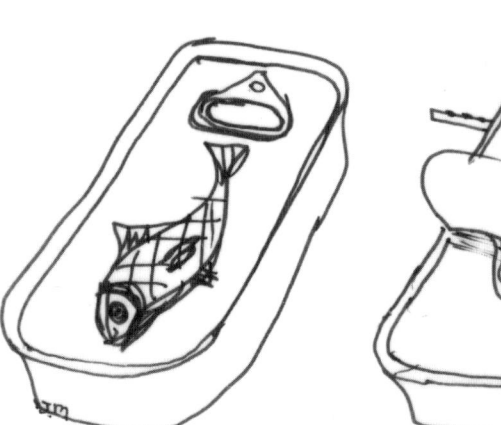

Holding the Flute

Centralising the Blowing

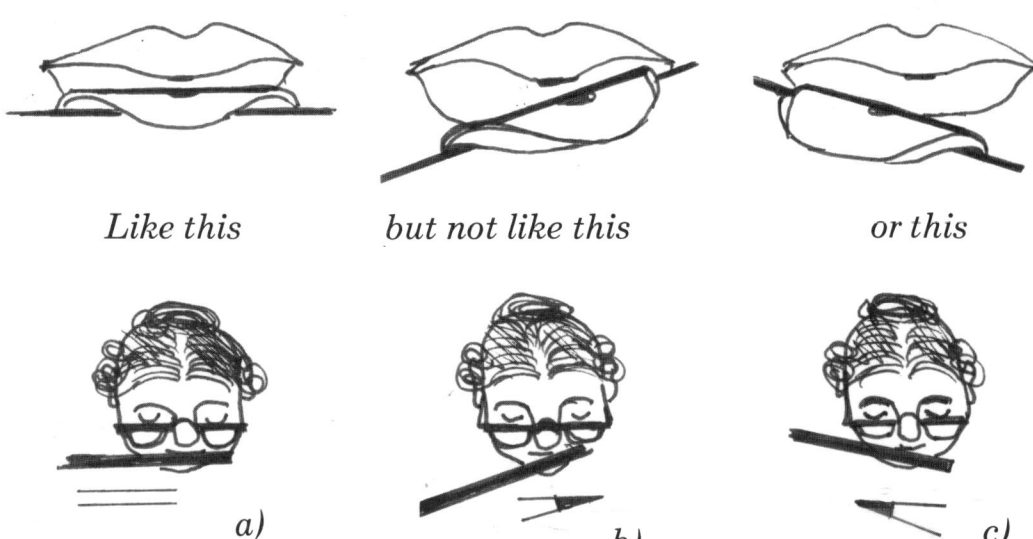

Like this   *but not like this*   *or this*

a)   b)   c)

Keep the flute exactly in line with your lips as in a) but not as in b) or c)

*Keep the flute **parallel** to your eyes and ears to ensure that the lip-plate is held evenly along your bottom lip so that your blowing can be correctly focused.*

*Line up flute and face **like this** with flute and head at right angles*

*but **not** like this with only head tilted*

*and **not** like this with only flute tilted.*

*These two positions would soon cause you to blow from the **side** of your mouth, off-centre, and the embouchure muscles would tend to become unbalanced, making fine control of tone and intonation that much more difficult.*

(You may, however, see some flute players who play beautifully even though they are apparently blowing off-centre and holding the flute awry — there are always exceptions to any rule!)

It's well worth checking all these holding angles in front of a long mirror, both standing and sitting; they will soon become automatic and natural, allowing you to play without tension and strain.

Posture

*Posture — the position you play in, either standing or sitting — makes a vital difference to breathing, tone, and technique. The posture of the **whole** body is important, not just the position of the head and arms.*

The flute is designed to be played at an angle; for comfort and ease the instrument must be held well away from the right shoulder, the head turned towards the left, the trunk and legs adjusting to accommodate this position.

Good posture standing

To practise holding the flute correctly, stand in a relaxed position, (1) imagine the flute is a recorder or clarinet, hold it pointing straight in front like a clarinettist, and bring it up to you (**don't go to IT**), (2) put it further up, by your left ear, (3) THEN turn your head to the flute, and pull the flute slightly towards your right arm, and TILT YOUR HEAD WITH THE FLUTE. It may help to lean back, putting your weight slightly more on the right leg than the left.

1 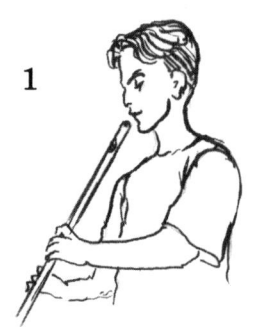   2 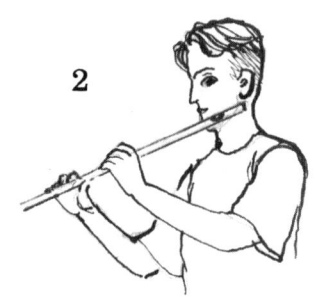   3

Posture 21

Group Playing

Whether standing or sitting in a group, make sure you keep a good posture to prevent straining your neck and shoulder muscles.

Remember: *(When **standing**)*

*"Left foot forward, right foot back,
Left shoulder forward, right shoulder back,
Flute behind your neighbour on the right-hand side,
Don't squash together, keep nice and wide".*

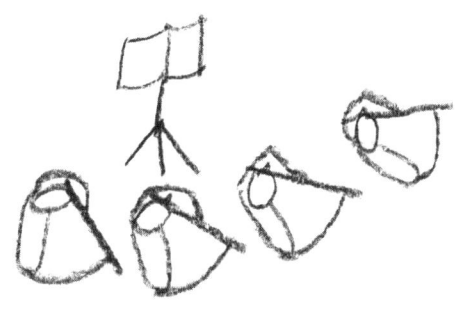

Four fluteplayers round one stand, viewed from above

When playing in an orchestra, position your chair and stand so that you can keep the correct posture and still see the conductor clearly. Your eyes, your music stand and the conductor should be in line, and the chair and your legs angled at about 45° to the right.

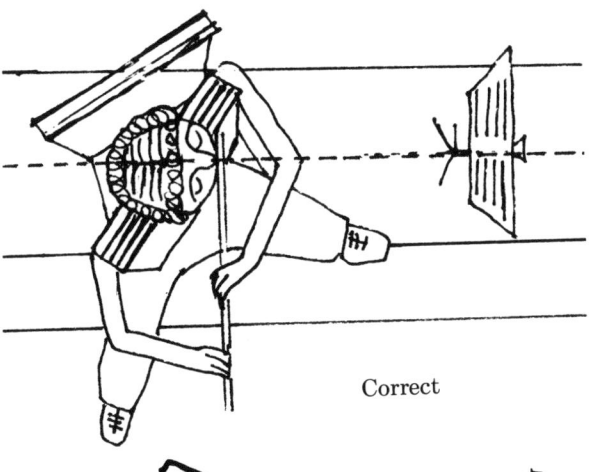

Correct

Fluteplayers in an orchestra, viewed from above.

To the conductor

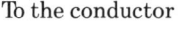

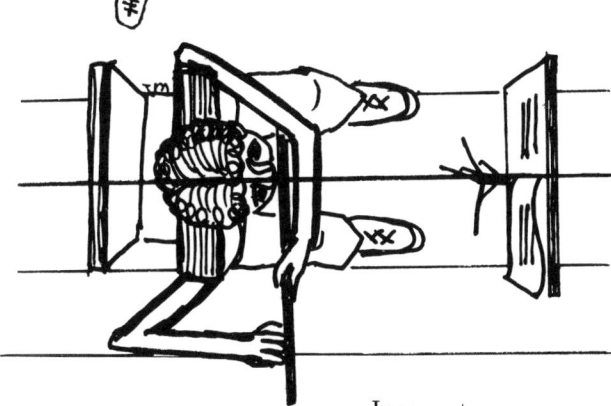

Incorrect

22   **Illustrated Fluteplaying**

This copy from a painting by Menzel shows King Frederick the Great of Prussia playing with a relaxed, natural posture.

For a well-balanced stance, which will allow you to breathe properly, and hold the flute at the correct angle

Either

Plant both feet firmly on the ground, a foot or so apart, with your weight equally distributed on each leg

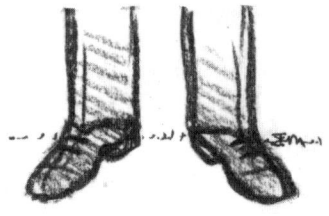

Correct

Or

Relax the left knee; lean weight mainly on right leg; put the left foot further forward than the right.

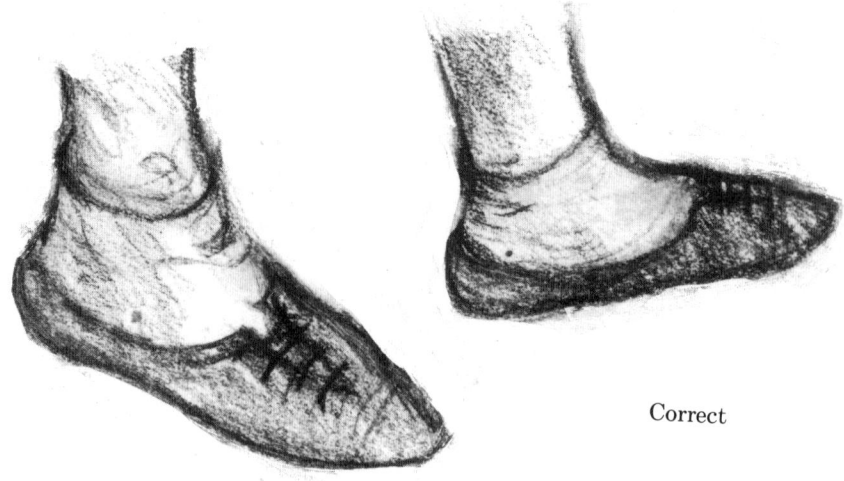

Correct

Posture

Some important DON'Ts for STANDING

*1. **Don't** cross your legs like a stork — you will be unbalanced, and breathing will be restricted.*

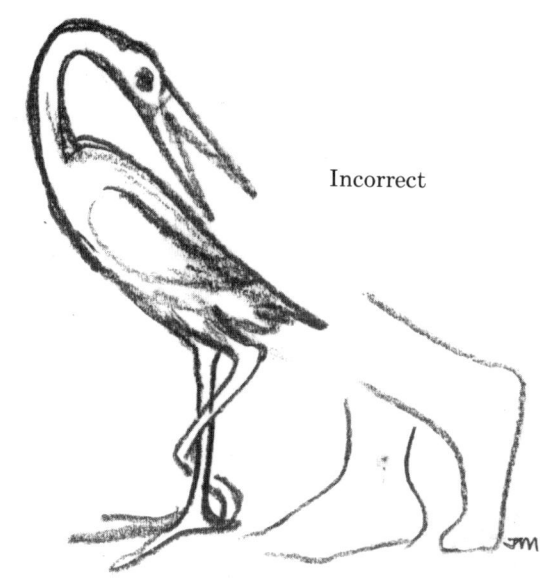
Incorrect

*2. **Don't** put **right** leg forward with weight on **left** — this twists the body awkwardly in relation to the flute, and blowing and breathing problems will probably develop.*

*3. **Don't** lean forward with hunched shoulders and a craning "tortoise" neck; your breathing will be affected, you will probably make a flat sound because you are blowing **down** too much, and the audience won't feel you are playing to them, but to the carpet! Remember (see page 20), always **bring the flute to you, don't go to IT**.*

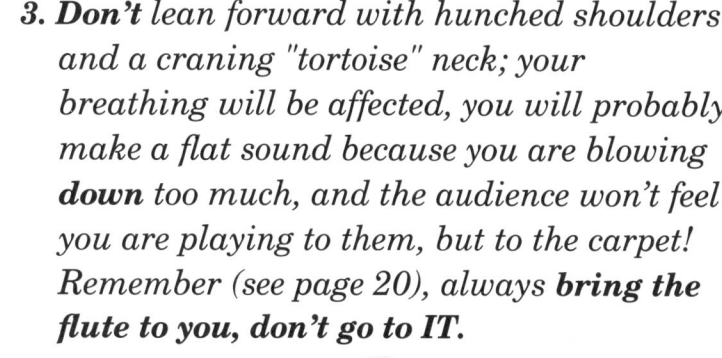
Incorrect

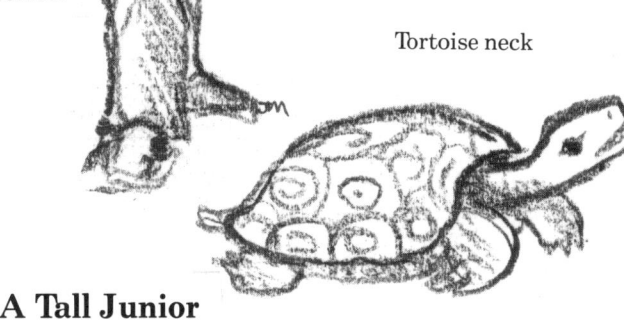
Tortoise neck — Incorrect

A Tall Junior

Some children who are quite tall for their age tend to stoop and stand badly (perhaps because they are trying to get down to the same level as their friends), and so may develop several bad habits in their playing that can be difficult to put right later (see page 75).

24 *Illustrated Fluteplaying*

Sitting

Correct

*For a comfortable sitting position that lets you **breathe** freely and also allows a good holding position that can be sustained for long periods without aches and pains developing:*

1. *Place your chair at 45° to the stand.*

2. *Swivel your trunk and shoulders towards the stand.*

3. *Keep your back straight, well away from the chair back.*

Notice angle of chair and stand.

Correct

*Your **flute** should be parallel to the stand.*

*Your **left elbow** should point towards the centre of the stand and your **left foot** should point to right of the stand.*

*You can then read the music properly (**and** see the conductor if any).*

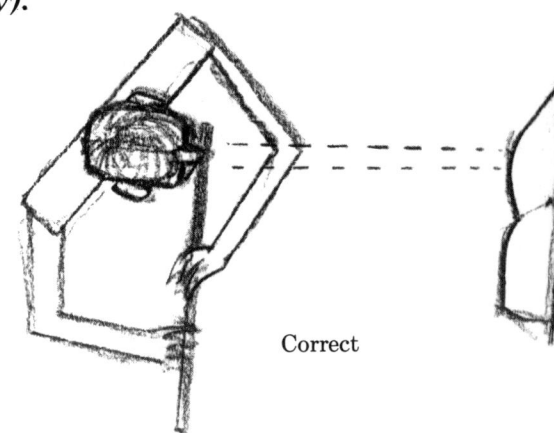

Correct

Some important DON'Ts for SITTING

1. **Don't** sit with the chair, your shoulders and the stand all parallel, or
   — *your left shoulder will begin to ache*
   — *your right-hand playing action will be cramped — the fingers will be unnecessarily curled*
   — *your breathing will be restricted.*
   These faults can inhibit your command over breathing, tone, intonation, and finger movement.

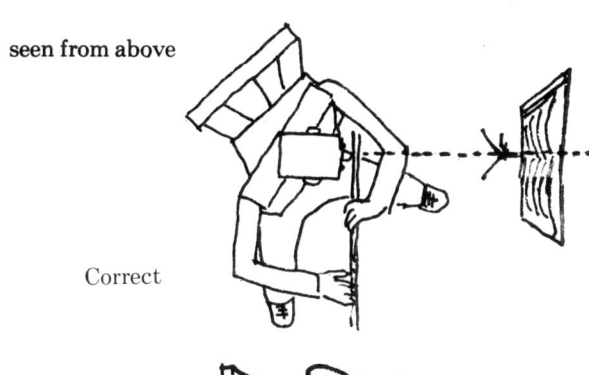

seen from above

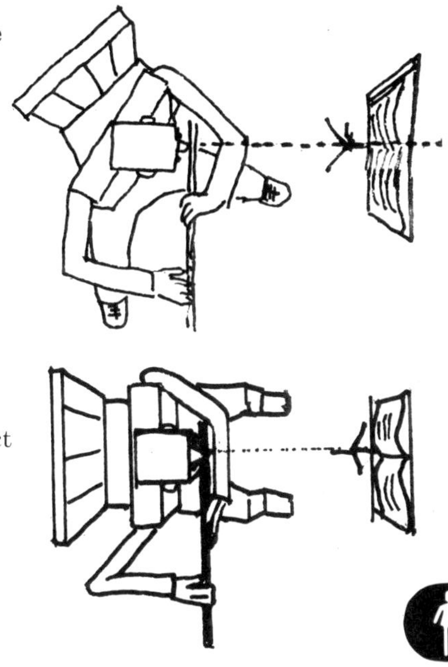

Correct

Incorrect

2. **Don't** lean against the back of your chair or you will restrict the action of the back muscles involved in correct breathing.

3. **Don't** be an **Arm Hooker**, hooking your right arm over the chair back: the playing muscles in your arm will be affected and the whole position of the body will be wrong.

Incorrect

4. **Don't** be a **Cross-Legged Sloucher** with a bowed back and drooping head.
   — *your breathing, tone, and tuning will all suffer.*

Incorrect

Hand Positions

Here are some drawings to show hand positions from different angles.

*Notice that the hands are held **below** the flute.*

*This means your wrists must be slightly **bent** at an angle to the arms (players vary in the amount of wrist-bending; in this book we illustrate quite a steep angle).*

After an engraving illustrating Hotteterre* Principes de la flûte traversière 1707

Good hand positions may seem a bit strange at first, but they will soon become natural, and allow for rapid and relaxed fingerwork.

the fingers retain their natural shape over the keys.

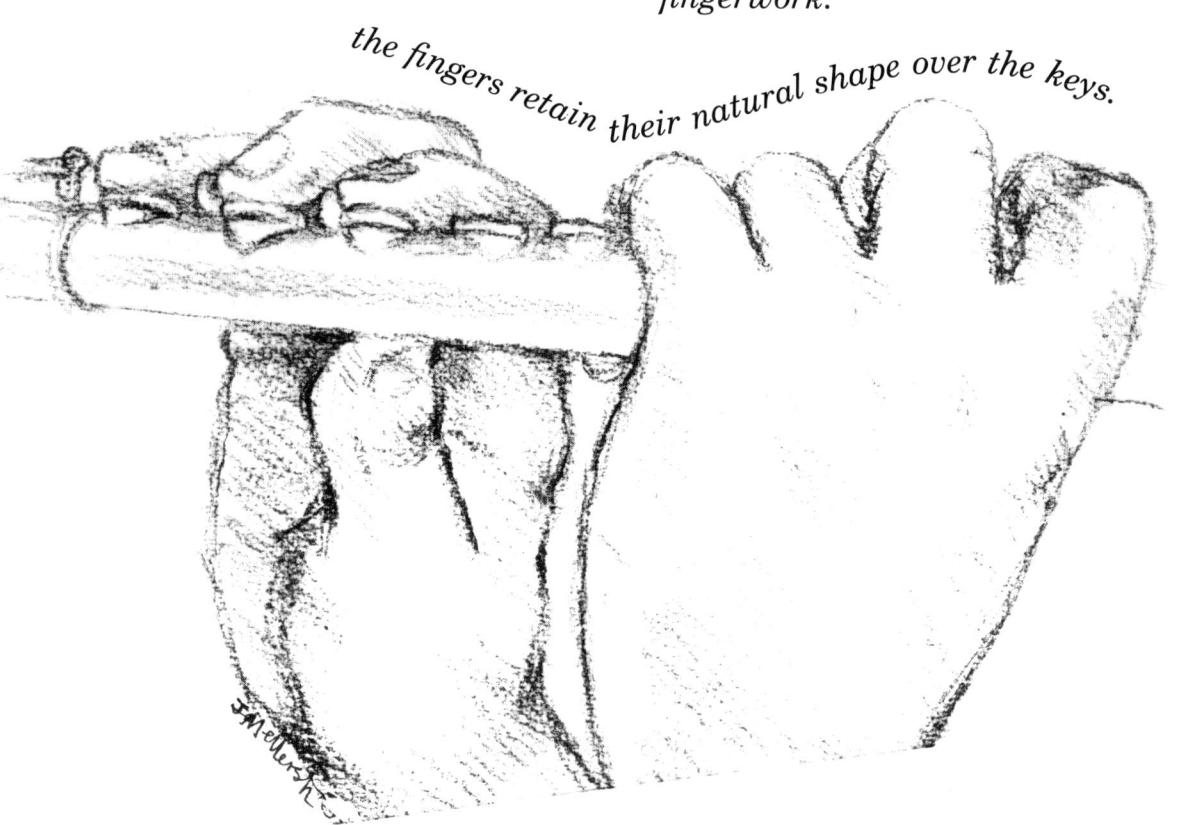

Hand Positions 27

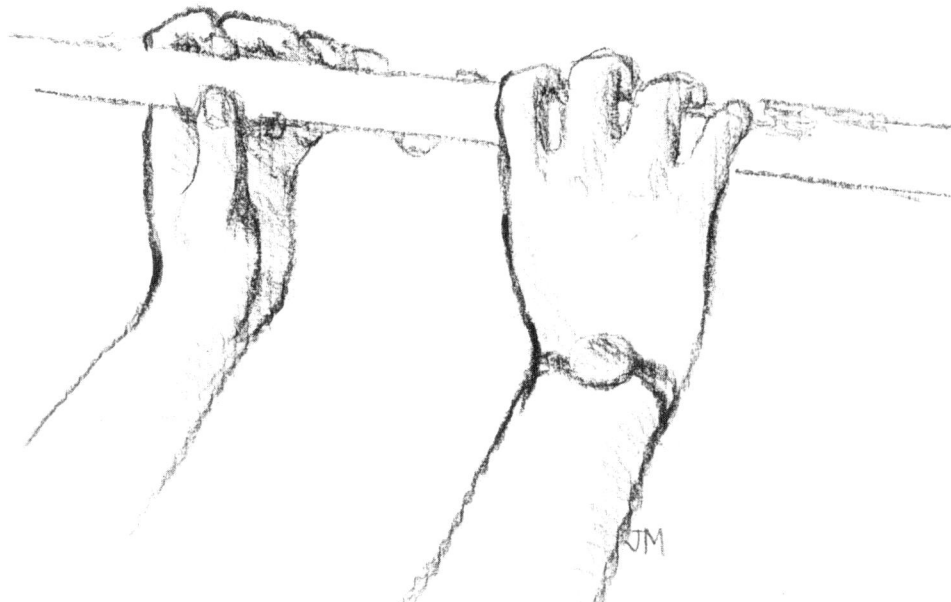

Remember —

Palms kept wide and free.

These hand positions bring the fingers evenly over the keys, so that only a very small finger movement is needed to press a key, and there is no jerkiness caused by snatching at a key from a distance.

Palms opened out flat, not creased or crumpled, with air spaces between each finger and around thumb especially at its base.

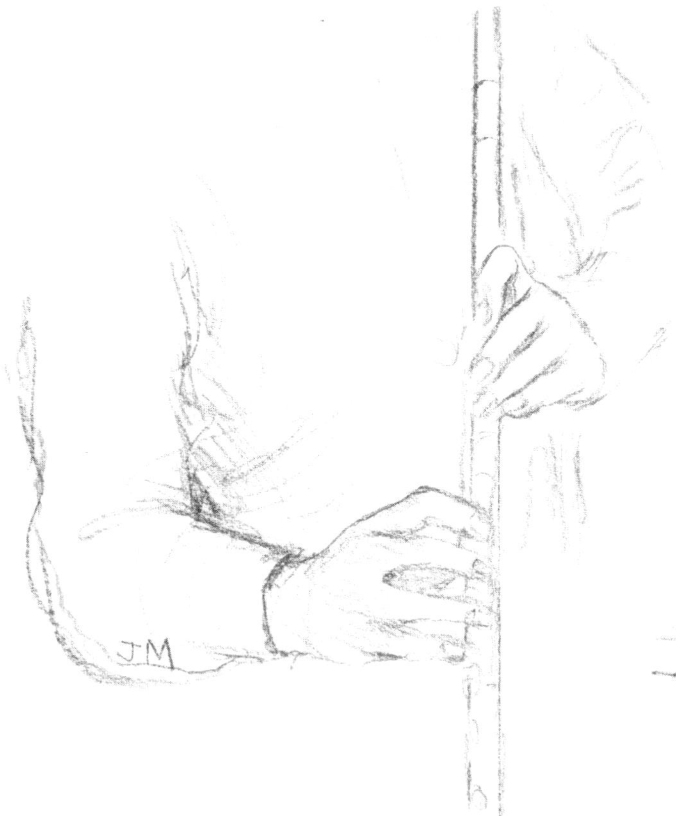

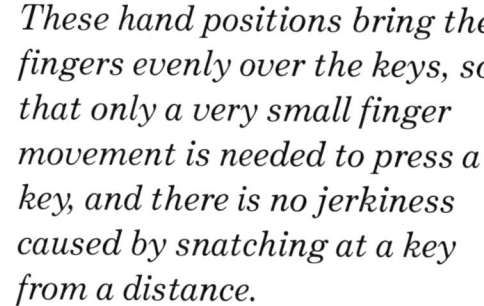

Illustrated Fluteplaying

The Fingers

The left index finger is placed at an angle to the flute.

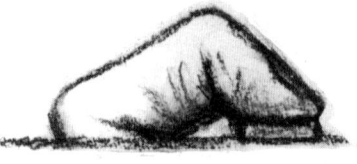

Correct   Both joints bent

The left index finger *should have two right angles in it. This allows the finger to move more freely, even though its lowest joint is a pressure point.*

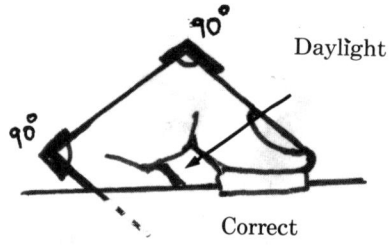

Correct

Incorrect   One joint straight

*The left middle, ring, and little fingers should be **curved** over the keys, not straight.*

Ideally the little finger should rest gently on the G sharp key or just above it. (Not dangling down or poking up).

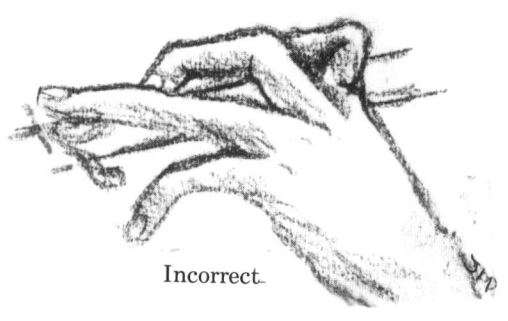

Incorrect

Hand Positions

Tips on Tips

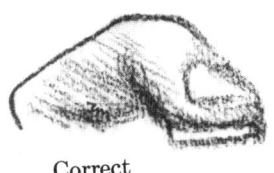
Correct

Incorrect

Incorrect

*Always place the fleshy **pads** of your fingers onto the centre of each key.*

*Imagine that the central depression of the key is an open hole. Make sure you cover it. Better still, get an open-hole flute one day (if you haven't already got one!)
You must hold and finger this type of flute correctly to play any notes at all.*

Make sure your key action itself is smooth, easy, and silent.

The movement is up and down, with no sliding off.

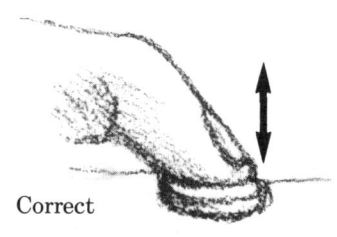
Correct

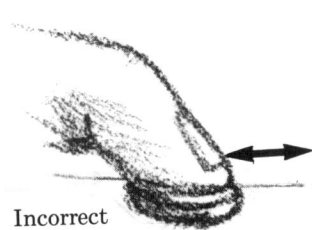
Incorrect

Speed and agility are needed for fingering, with strong fingers that can be totally under control and moved with complete precision.

Whatever the speed or dynamics of the music, finger and key action should be silent (unless percussive clicks on keys are called for by the composer).

Remember, very little pressure is needed to press the keys. Fast or loud playing makes no difference to pressure needed.

30 *Illustrated Fluteplaying*

The Left Hand — *Correct Position*

*Keep your thumb **straight** and at 90° to the flute, forming a "T".*
Keep thumb high on the key.
This will allow the fingers to come over the keys as naturally as possible — the left wrist will need to bend a bit, depending on the size of your hand.

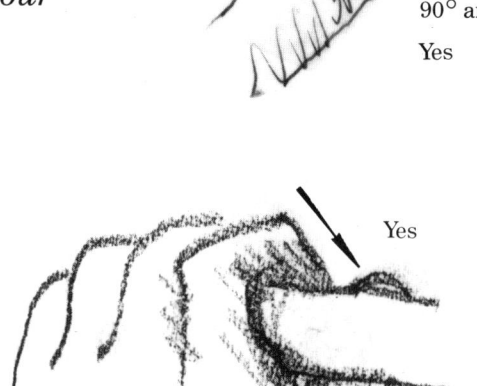
90° angle
Yes

If you have a long thumb, the end of it may show from in front.

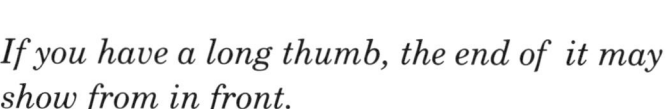
Yes

You can see daylight through here

and here.

Left Hand Fingering Faults

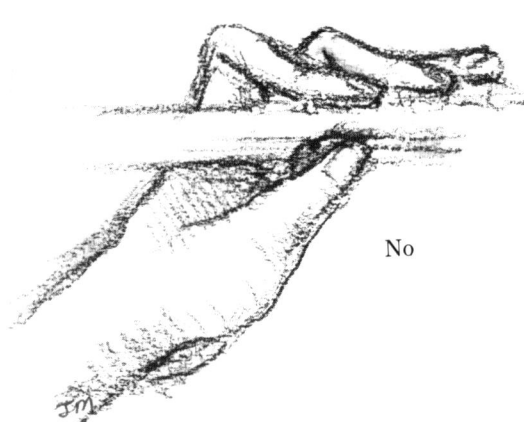
No

Straight wrist, pulling ring and little fingers away from keys.

*If your thumb is **bent**, or comes onto the thumb-key from the left, the ring and little fingers will be pulled away from their keys.*

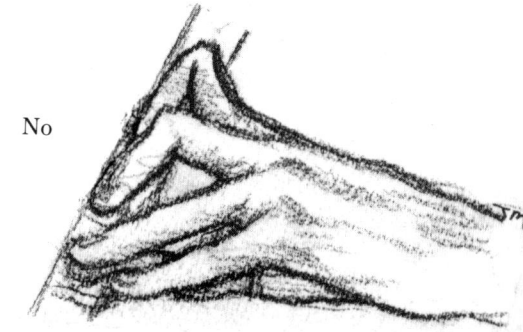
No

Hand Positions

The Right Hand-*Correct Position*

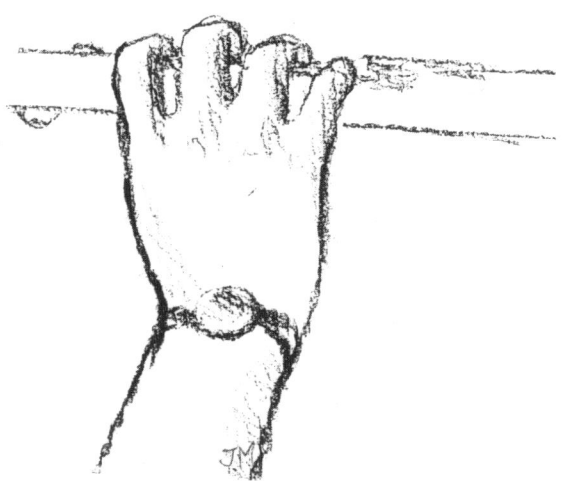

*The little finger is **bent**. Both joints need to retain their natural curve. Always use little finger on its **side**.*

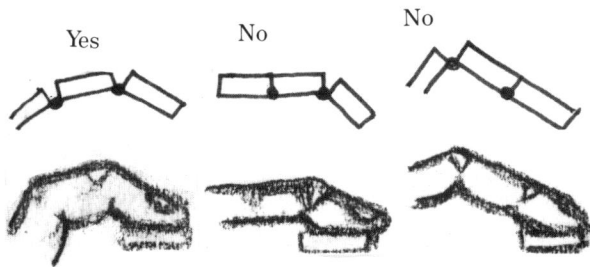

Right Hand Fingering Faults

Straight Little Finger
This tends to lift the wrist and push the hand to the left, making it very difficult to use the C, C sharp and E flat keys correctly. You are forced to alter your hand positions as you play these low notes. There are also tensions in the muscles.

*This simple experiment will explain the correct position for the right hand: hang your arm loosely by your side. Shake your hand around as though you want to ensure good circulation in the fingers. Lift your hand and look at it — the thumb is on its **side**, the fingers are all slightly curved. Put your hand to the flute in exactly this position, with the thumb **end** pushing against the flute, **behind** it, not **under** it. The little finger must remain curved. This position is absolutely essential for relaxed playing. Neither **raise** your wrist too high, nor drop it too low.*

*Imagine you are about to catch a tennis ball thrown from a distance to your shoulder height. If you put your thumb **under** the flute and/or straighten your little finger, the other fingers will be twisted away from the instrument, causing many problems of evenness in technique.*

Some people have very loose joints; the little finger often straightens — one cure is to ensure the wrist position is correct and not twisted.

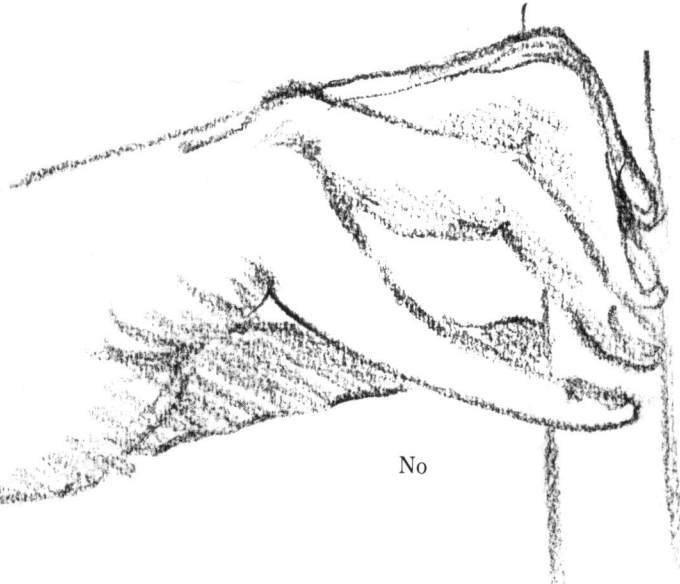

No

Illustrated Fluteplaying

"Parrot Fingers"

*The fingers are bent awkwardly over the keys (like a parrot's claws) and their tips touch the keys rather than the **pads**. This cramps the muscles and prevents a smooth finger action.*

Incorrect

"Thumb Poker"

*Poking your thumb causes problems: the thumb is not able to push the flute in its job as **a pressure point**, so the right fingers tend to **squash against the rods** to help hold the flute steady. This prevents smooth finger-action on the keys.*

Hand Positions   33

"Banana Fingers"

The fingers droop over the keys like bananas. Usually this is a result of "thumb poking" and lifting right wrist. The fingers usually rest on the rods and their movement is constricted.

Incorrect

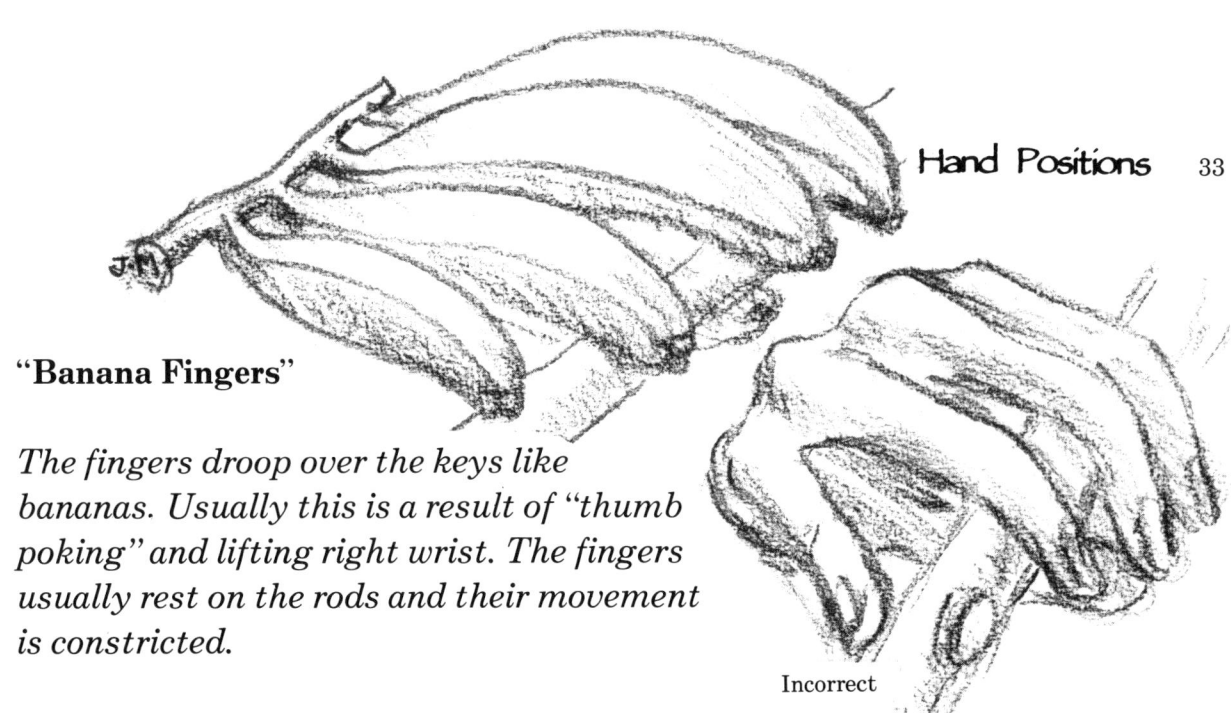

"Vicar's Tea Party" Fingers

The ring finger and little finger of both hands tend to fly about elegantly but inefficiently a long way above the keys. The finger movement is uneven and fast playing is very difficult.

Incorrect

Shoulders & Elbows

Correct

Always drop the shoulders when you play. Dropped shoulders usually indicate correct breathing and go with a good posture.

Incorrect

Shoulders raised, head craning forward, neck aches, and bad tuning results!

Raised shoulders are often the result of starting to play the flute very young (under 10), when the length and the weight of the instrument causes the child to rest the flute onto the left shoulder. This can become a habit that causes a lot of problems later on. There are flutes with a bent headjoint, designed for very young flute players, which help to eliminate this problem. (See page 74.) Many young players now start on inexpensive plastic fifes which are short, light, and easy to learn to blow.

Incorrect

Shoulders and Elbows 35

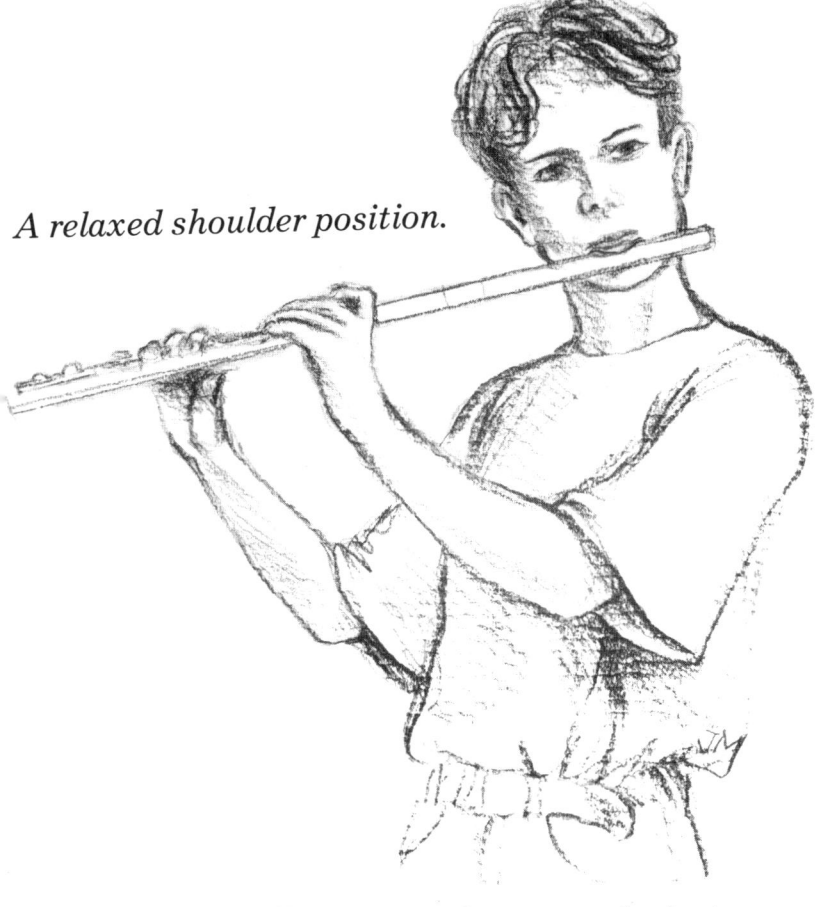

A relaxed shoulder position.

*Keep your elbows **away** from your body (to allow correct breathing and hand positions), but not too high or the angle of the flute on the mouth will alter and affect tone and tuning.*

Elbows too high.

*Try not to be an **elbow waggler**. Keep your elbows **still** while you play. If you move your elbows up (especially the left one) as you go up the register; you create more tuning problems (see page 71) and you are likely to play with a thinner tone at the top.*

Elbows too close to body.

Tonguing

*Every time you blow a note on the flute (when you are learning to make a good sound), you should first take a good breath (as described on page 46, 47), and feel all the exhaling muscles pushing a strong air stream against the resistance created by the embouchure. Practise short repeated notes making a firm attack on each note, as in saying **"Huh, huh, huh"** making a deliberately violent inward tummy movement for each note. This action (less violent usually)* **is really 90% of the work involved in tonguing!** *The tonguing movement described on page 37 is merely a final addition to this attack from the breath.*

Think of the tongue action as a bit like a flag waving in the breeze —

*and **not** as a series of short bursts, as in morse code.*

Tongue Movement Routine

*The tongue is needed to make a clear, more precise **beginning** to the note, not as woolly or vague as in "huh" or "phoo", more like "too" or "doo".*

Practise this routine, blowing first across your finger (as on page 5).

1. *Take a good breath.*
2. *Form your embouchure.*
3. *Blow a continuous air-jet (not tonguing)*

*Now repeat 1 and 2 but **add** the tonguing movement to the continuous air-jet.*

One commonly used method

The tongue movement varies considerably from one player to another but to start with,

While continuously blowing:

a. *Place tip of tongue gently against the roof of your mouth just behind the upper gums (the palate).*

b. *Withdraw tip of tongue into mouth cavity.*

c. *Replace tip of tongue against palate.*

*This action gives a "too" or "doo" kind of sound, although these words are not actually **said**; it's just the **feel** of pronouncing them that matters.*

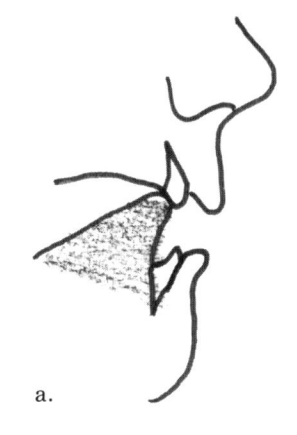

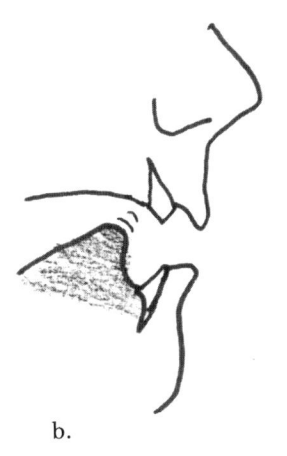

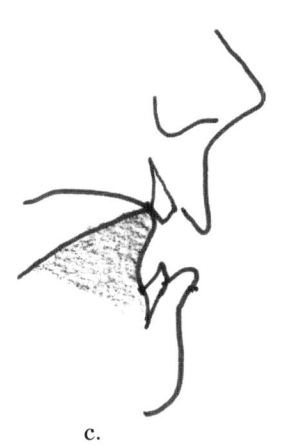

Illustrated Fluteplaying

Here are some other common ways of starting the tongue action.

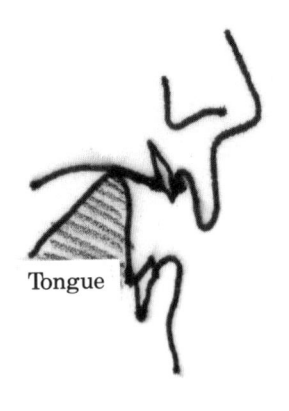

1

*Tongue rests **further back** against roof of mouth. Often used for very rapid tonguing and especially for double tonguing.*

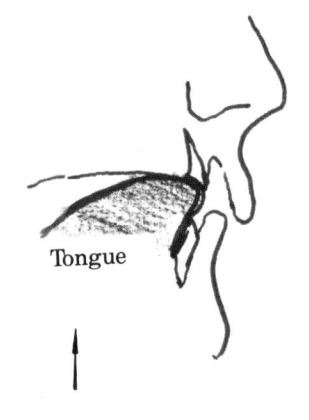

2

*Tongue rests between **teeth**. This can be very clear and positive.*

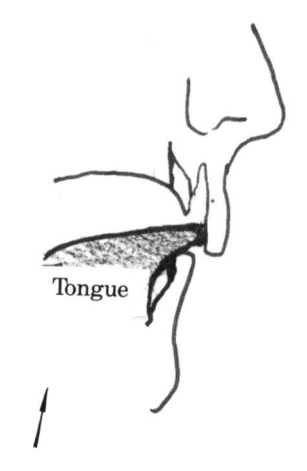

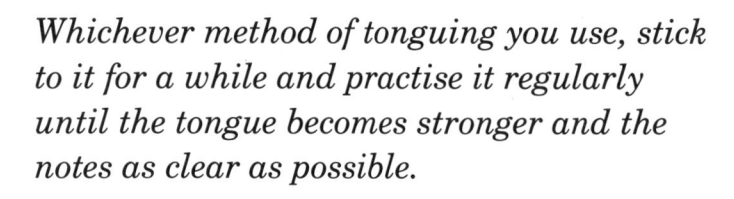

3

*Tongue rests against **top lip**. This method can be a good way of playing with a harder, very precise and more accented attack. This is usually called **Forward** or **Popping** tonguing. Many players prefer method 3 (Forward tonguing), as it is possible to produce a sparkling staccato and vibrantly clear fast passages in this way.*

Whichever method of tonguing you use, stick to it for a while and practise it regularly until the tongue becomes stronger and the notes as clear as possible.

These methods all produce slightly different sounds for the start of the note, and it is eventually useful to be able to tongue in several different ways to suit the music.

Tonguing

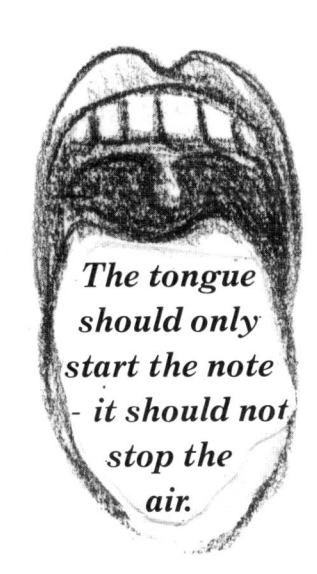

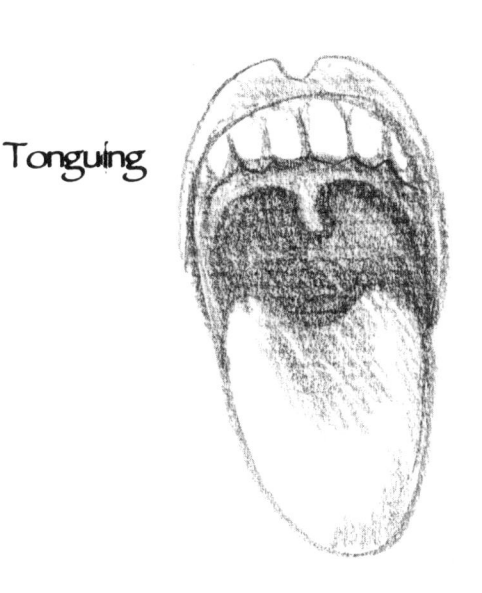

The tongue should only start the note - it should not stop the air.

With the headjoint, play gently **"too, too, too"** or **"doo, doo, doo"**, checking that you are moving a continuous air stream while you tongue.

To obtain a delicate and even tonguing action, practise in an easy scale repeating each note four times and pausing between each note.

First **not** tonguing (but feeling "huh, huh"). Then with tongue, but maintaining a strong abdominal pressure.

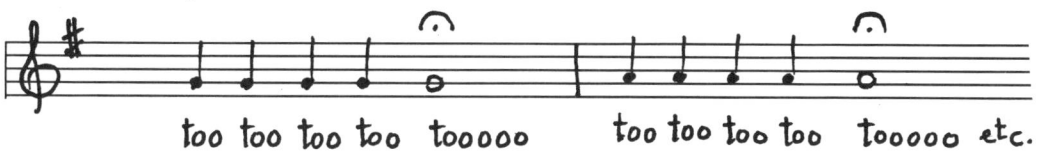

too too too too tooooo   too too too too tooooo etc.

Do this **very softly** at first, as playing loudly may cause the tongue to move rather violently when you are learning. Remember, **both** soft and **loud** playing require the same accuracy and delicacy from the tongue.

Most tonguing difficulties are caused by **overdoing** the tongue movement and trying too hard! The tongue muscle will gradually strengthen until just the **tip** of the tongue is moved a **small** distance inside the mouth, and tonguing becomes effortless (and very rapid, if required).

Whatever method you use, keep your throat open

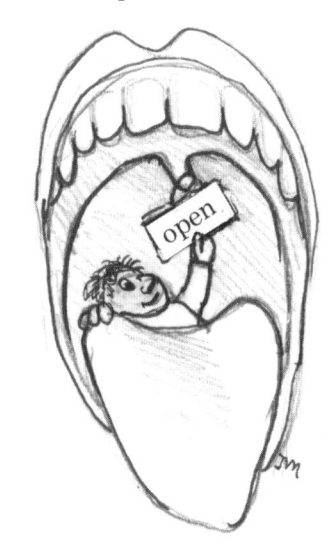

40 *Illustrated Fluteplaying*

Part II

Breathing

Breathing properly is the most important part of playing any wind instrument, and this is particularly so with the flute. Unlike its neighbours in the orchestra (the oboe, clarinet, and bassoon), the flute has no reed, nor has it a small aperture or mouthpiece to blow through. In reed instruments the very small opening between the reed and mouthpiece as in the clarinet, or between the double reeds in the oboe and bassoon, creates a built-in resistance. Players of this kind of instrument can sustain their playing for long periods, often having to get rid of unused "stale" air in their lungs before taking another breath. It would be difficult for a flute player to play for equally long periods in one breath because the instrument itself doesn't provide much resistance at all; there is no reed to vibrate, only a fixed edge to blow against.

A player has to control the flow of air and its strength and speed entirely with the muscles of his embouchure and breathing apparatus. Most beginners find themslves running out of breath after a few moments because they can't yet control these muscles properly — the air comes rushing out all over the place. Very often they tend to blow too hard, and the lack of control makes them feel dizzy, and the sound produced (if any!) is weak, woolly and unfocused.

It is most important to understand that you never need to blow really hard to get the flute to "speak" either for very soft or very loud playing. What happens when you blow a note is that the molecules of air already in the flute get "excited" by the turbulence caused by the activity of the air-jet and they bump into each other in a particular way so that the whole column of air in the instrument vibrates. Most of the air comes out of the blow hole, **hardly any of the air comes out of the tone holes or the foot end** (in fact, the amount is so small it can be ignored). Blowing the flute is not like blowing a pea-shooter: you don't blow **through** the instrument, you "drive" it by the fine control of the air-jet, which acts as the "motor". In an oboe the double reed is the motor; in a flute it is the air-jet. A good player shows that it's not the **amount** of air you blow that makes a beautiful sound, but the **control** of the size, speed and direction of the air-jet. This control is closely linked to correct breathing.

Breathing 43

Most people only use a very small fraction of their total lung capacity for ordinary "everyday" breathing — we breathe in a smooth, quiet, effortless way that obviously requires no conscious thought. When we need to burn more oxygen during some strenuous physical activity we instinctively use the appropriate muscles to inflate the lungs more fully, and this again is a natural, built-in process. If you go for a quick run and then stand still, out of breath, consider what's happening: you pant heavily, mouth open, with a heaving chest and expanding tummy and lower back area, drawing as much air in as possible to adjust to the body's needs.

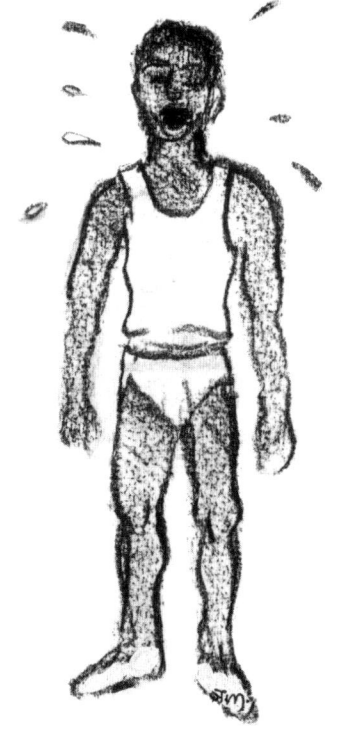

Flute-playing is not usually regarded as a strenuous physical activity, but correct blowing requires so much breath control that the same areas of muscle that come to the rescue automatically after a run must be called on to support the air supply. At first this must be learned, and done in a conscious way. You may see a good player looking completely relaxed and playing with hardly any apparent effort, but he will nevertheless be using the whole range of breathing muscles (without thinking about them) to make the flute respond. Only after a while does this deeper breathing become as natural as "everyday" breathing, letting you switch to "automatic pilot" for breathing, to concentrate on the music. At first you must also concentrate on what is happening to each bit of your body as you breathe, to check that it's doing the proper job with the whole body involved in breathing, not just the lungs.

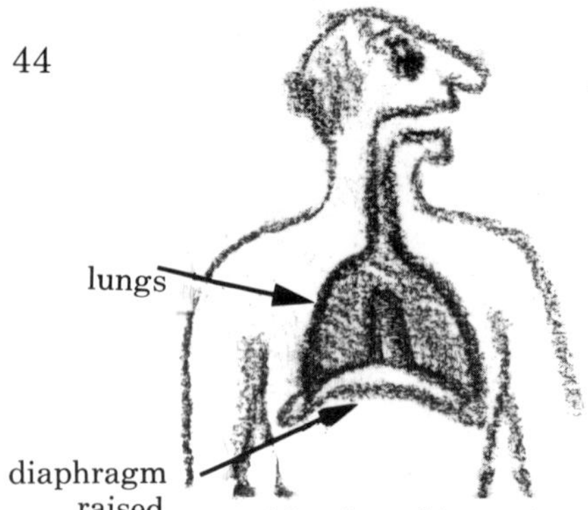

Illustrated Fluteplaying

lungs
diaphragm raised
After breathing out

This simplified diagram shows the most important parts of the body that control breathing:

Notice the position of the **diaphragm.** The diaphragm is, roughly speaking, a muscular sheet separating the **thorax** (which contains the rib-cage and lungs) from the **abdomen** or belly. The thorax and abdomen are two sealed compartments; there is no connection between them, the diaphragm being the seal. In deep breathing the diaphragm can be moved down so that it acts like a piston or plunger inside the body.

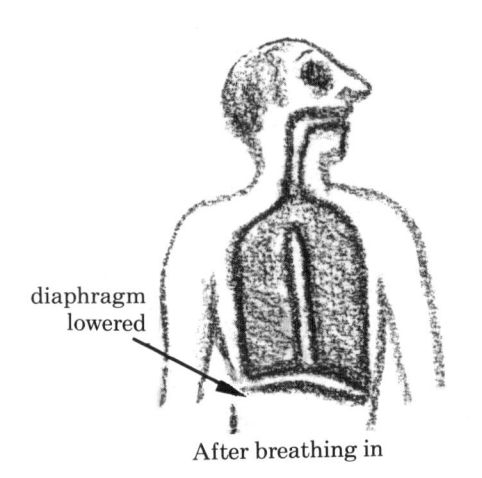

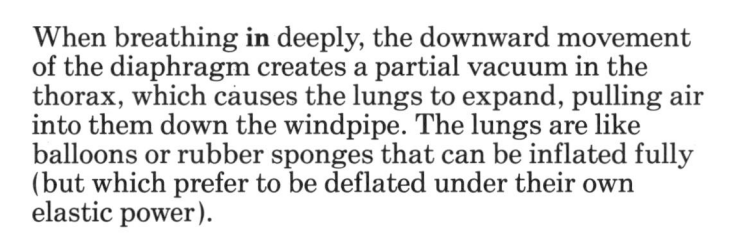

diaphragm lowered
After breathing in

When breathing **in** deeply, the downward movement of the diaphragm creates a partial vacuum in the thorax, which causes the lungs to expand, pulling air into them down the windpipe. The lungs are like balloons or rubber sponges that can be inflated fully (but which prefer to be deflated under their own elastic power).

When breathing **out**, the diaphragm returns to its usual position, and there is no longer any vacuum in the cavity of the thorax, so the lungs deflate under their own elasticity, and air is expelled through the windpipe.

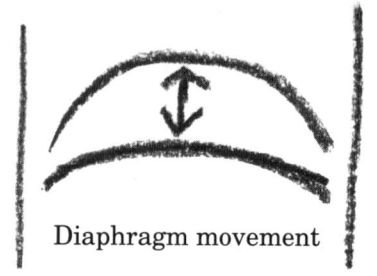

Diaphragm movement

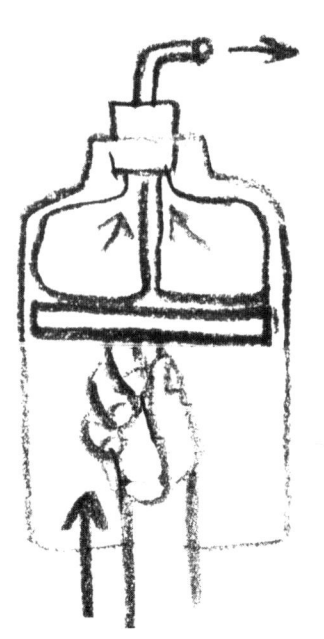

Plunger moves up as air is exhaled

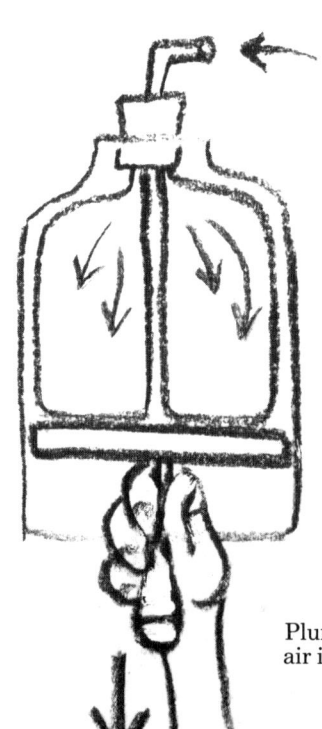

Plunger moves down as air is inhaled

Although we also use many other muscles to control breathing, this plunger-like movement of the diaphragm is by far the most important factor. The trouble is, you can't see the diaphragm like you can see your belly or chest muscles — you only know you're using it properly by the way in which it affects other areas. Sneezing, coughing, laughing or crying are activities that call on help from the diaphragm. You can also feel yourself breathing with the diaphragm if you go for a run and then, standing still and straight, concentrate on breathing while keeping everything in your body **completely still**, including your belly and chest: the diaphragm will be working hard to keep the airflow going. (If it didn't, you would be dead).

You can also try lying down, holding the chest still, and watch your abdomen rise and fall with each breath. As the diaphragm descends for the intake of air it pushes the contents of the abdomen out of the way (things like the liver, stomach, gall bladder), and this causes the elasticated walls around your midriff to push outwards. When you breathe out, the upward movement of the diaphragm allows the abdomen to return to its previous position and the tummy-area moves inwards. So it is important to let the abdominal muscles remain **relaxed** while you breathe in, to allow the diaphragm to push the abdomen contents out of the way. If you try to breathe in using the "tummy muscles" (the muscles used in sit-up exercises), you constrict the movement of the diaphragm and so prevent enough air from entering the lungs. Of course, the muscles round the tummy, midriff and back area are used to help support the expansion of your body as you breathe in, and the chest muscles and the muscles between the ribs are also important, but secondary to the main control, the action of the diaphragm, so abdomen muscles are supportive but not rock-hard.

46 *Illustrated Fluteplaying*

Here is a bit more detail about the breathing process.

Breathing IN

To breathe in, breathe through the mouth, not the nose (unless you are advanced enough to practise "circular breathing"), keeping a relaxed, open throat, as in yawning, or in saying a silent "aahh", but not as in gargling.

Open throat

as in yawning

but not as in gargling

There are really three stages to breathing in, each one following rapidly after the one before. Start the intake of air from the tummy area, and build it up from there.

Stage 1
Relax the tummy area, and allow it to be pushed downwards to expand in all directions as the diaphragm descends, just as if you are "dropping" it.

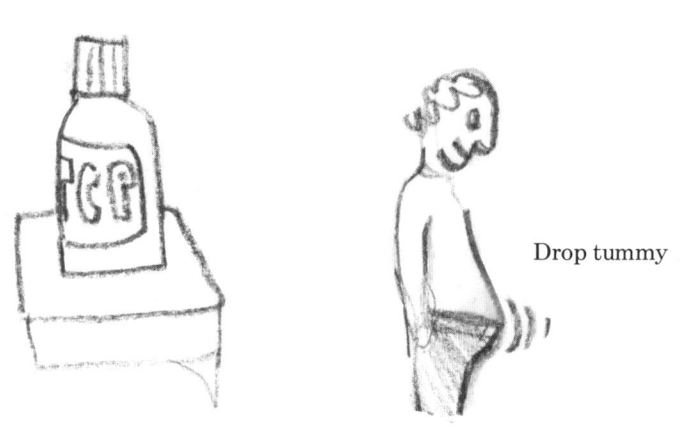

Drop tummy

Make sure your belt is not too tight, as this restricts the tummy movement, and don't eat a huge meal just before playing, because a full stomach stops the downward movement of the diaphragm. (If, at the other extreme you are dying of hunger, you will tend to feel weak and faint during deep breathing, so be sensible and time your meals to feel comfortable but not full up.)

Stage 2
Allow the abdominal muscles to expand round your midriff and back area, at the same time pulling the tummy back in and firming the muscles round it to get a feeling of strong support round the whole midriff area.

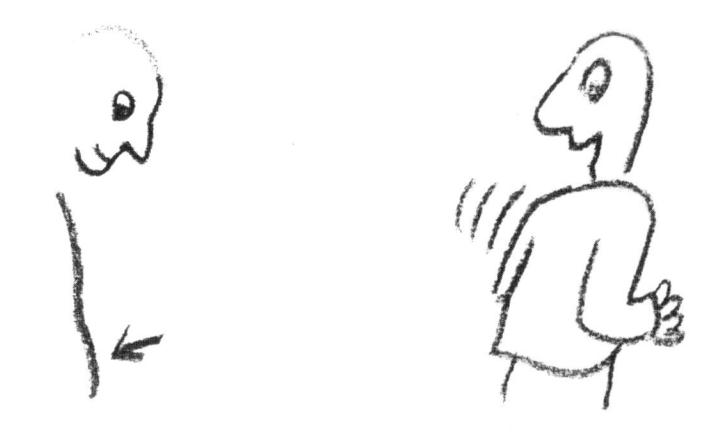

Stage 3
Expand your chest and let your rib cage expand to the fullest extent, rather like expanding a concertina:

These three stages should be performed virtually together, the whole process only taking a moment, but make sure that the sequence is correct, so that the intake of breath starts from below and builds up. In this way the lungs can be inflated most rapidly and efficiently.

Remember — never tighten the throat, but allow a large volume of air to pass down the windpipe quite freely:
- keep your shoulders low, wide and relaxed
- keep a good posture

(see pages 20 – 25).

48 **_Illustrated Fluteplaying_**

correct posture
goes with
correct breathing

Incorrect
Military posture
One of the surest give-away signs of inefficient breathing is the "military" posture, like a soldier on parade:
— the shoulders lift
— the tummy pulls in
— the chest puffs out
— the head is held too far back

This posture is often mistakenly taken to be the only correct method of taking a "big breath", but in fact it is almost impossible to inflate the lungs effectively in this way, mainly because the diaphragm cannot do its work efficiently. If you try to blow the flute after breathing in like this you are almost certain to produce a feeble sound, and can only play short, snatched phrases and furthermore, it's extremely **tiring** to breathe this way. Correct breathing should always be as **effortless** as possible.

Unfortunately, many children brought up in the classical ballet tradition may often be told to stand with belly in, shoulders high - (the opposite of the correct method of breathing for the flute).

Breathing

Breathing OUT

Think of breathing out as a wave of air rising inside your body, so that the exhalation starts low down in the abdomen, with the air pushing out progressively higher up, rather like toothpaste squeezing up from the bottom of the tube until it's empty.

As you breathe out, the upward movement of the diaphragm allows all the naturally "elastic" parts of the breathing mechanism to return to their "normal" or passive positions: the tummy and midriff, the back muscles, and the muscles in the chest. The muscles between the ribs all contract, and the lungs deflate under their own elastic power to provide the outward flow of air. This air flow is put under pressure by the resistance created by the embouchure, so that the smaller the lip-aperture, the greater the pressure. This can be compared to stopping a garden hose with your thumb: the more the hose is stopped the faster and further the water travels.

The air-jet is controlled in the same way, so that it varies in speed and strength according to the size of the lip-aperture.

The outward pressure of air has to be perfectly balanced and controlled **inside** your body, with the diaphragm once again the main fine-tuning mechanism and all the other muscles we have mentioned acting as secondary supports.

50 *Illustrated Fluteplaying*

To sum up

This method of breathing in sequence, using the diaphragm together with the supporting muscles, should be practised until it becomes quite natural. Some suggested exercises are illustrated on page 53. If you always make an effort to fill the **base** of the lungs first, the rest of the breathing process almost looks after itself. As with a bicycle pump, good pumping starts with the plunger at its fullest extent.

A musical passage often only allows a fraction of a second for breathing in, and the breathing action in this case may be quite violent, like the shocked intake of air when you jump into a freezing lake, or get a pin stuck into you. The diaphragm moves down very rapidly, and the abdominal and back muscles expand energetically. For a more relaxed breath, the intake of air can be almost inaudible although the same process is used.

Shocked intake of air

In the end, we don't have to **think** about any of these breathing processes; the body responds in a natural way to the demands of the music, and breathing simply becomes part of the music. The music itself seems to breathe, and we are not aware of the playing effort — a really good player never appears to breathe.

Shocked intake of air

Breathing 51

Posture for breathing

Correct posture is vital to let all these movements be made easily and naturally, whether standing or sitting;

Keep your head and neck erect to avoid constrictions in the throat and allow the maximum resonance.

Imagine that you are a puppet and your head is being pulled upwards and each bone in your spine is being lifted off the one below.

Imagine you are a hamster with nuts in your cheeks as you play the high notes.

The cavities in the throat, nose, and mouth area play a part in bringing a **resonance** to the sound so that, as in singing, a flute player can use all the available resonating areas. A thin or lifeless sound is often caused by tightening up the throat and cheeks instead of letting air remain inside these areas.

The chest and vocal chords must also be allowed to resonate for a really full and carrying sound.

(Further information can be found in the chapter entitled "Throat Tuning" in Robert Dick's book "Tone Development through Extended Techniques").

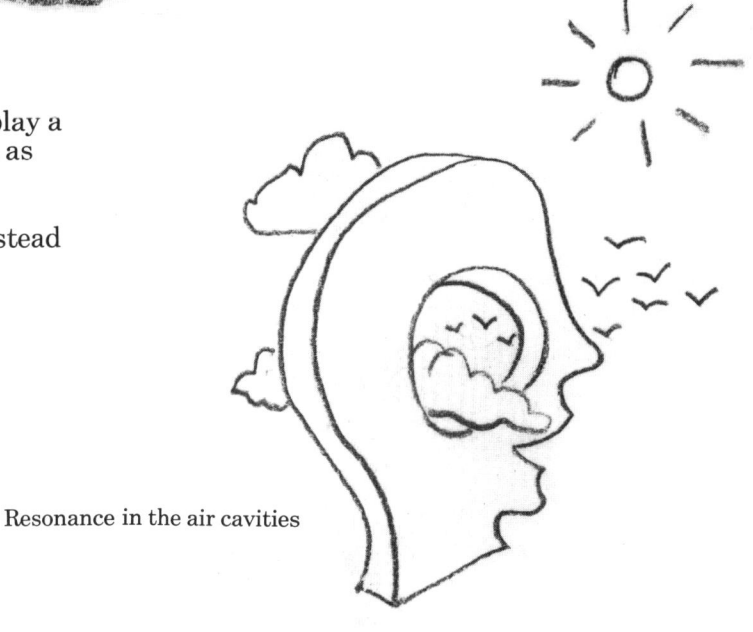

Resonance in the air cavities

52 *Illustrated Fluteplaying*

When standing make sure your **hips** are more or less horizontal in relation to the floor so that the pelvis doesn't poke into the body areas that you need for breathing!

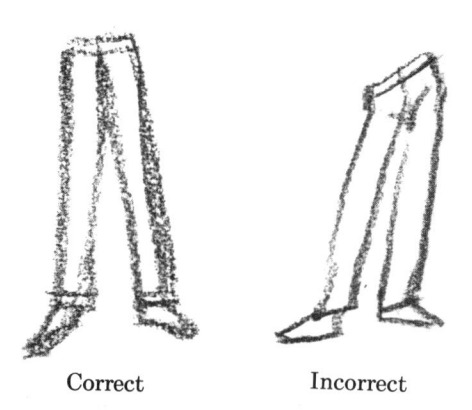

Correct   Incorrect

A correct **seated** posture is even more critical for good breathing — keep your back straight, and **well away** from the back of the chair so that the muscles in the small of your back and chest can expand freely. Don't slouch or cross your legs, and avoid twisting the abdomen awkwardly.

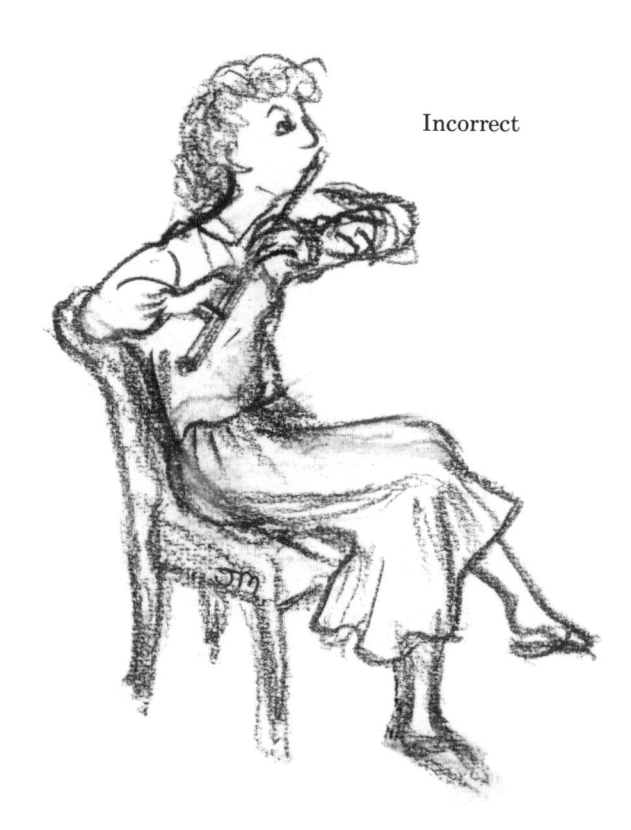

Correct   Incorrect

Breathing exercises

Here are some exercises to help develop good breathing:

Stand feet apart, hands below knees, breathe to expand your back.

Sit comfortably. Relax forward, arms on knees, legs apart, breathe, expanding your back.

Place one end of flute case on abdomen, the other end against a heavy piece of furniture. Breathe out and you tilt forward. Breathe in as you are swayed back.

Check your tummy movements by pressing the flute firmly against your navel and breathing in against this pressure. Try to make the outward movement at least 3 or 4 inches.

Dynamics & Tuning

Changing Pitch and Dynamics and Playing in Tune

In this guide the same, very subtle movements of the "Three Controls" are used both for helping to change pitch (for example, jumping octaves) and for playing in tune at different dynamics.

Changing pitch

If you take an octave leap that uses the same fingering (such as low F to middle F, low G to middle G, and so on) and simply blow harder, the upper octave note is breathy, unfocused, and probably sharp. You might get the octave leap by rolling the flute in, but the note is most likely to be thin and very flat.

To jump an octave, **never blow harder**
never roll the flute in or out

You don't need more breath to play high notes — all you have to do is increase the **speed** of the air-jet and not its volume. A faster air speed produces the octave above (the first harmonic) without any real effort if small adjustments are made to the three controls. This faster air speed is created by making the lip-gap smaller (like the garden hose stopped with the thumb, see page 15, 49). The more the lip-gap is closed the faster the same volume of air has to travel. The top lip acts like the thumb on the hose; it is the main valve which presses down onto the air-jet and puts the jet under more pressure.

Note
The top lip is actually **pulled down** rather than being "pushed" from the top, as all muscular action is produced by a "pulling" action.

This fact partly explains why a smiley embouchure makes a good downward pull by these muscles more difficult; there is a conflict between the downward pull and the upward pull of the smile. A straighter bottom lip solves this problem.

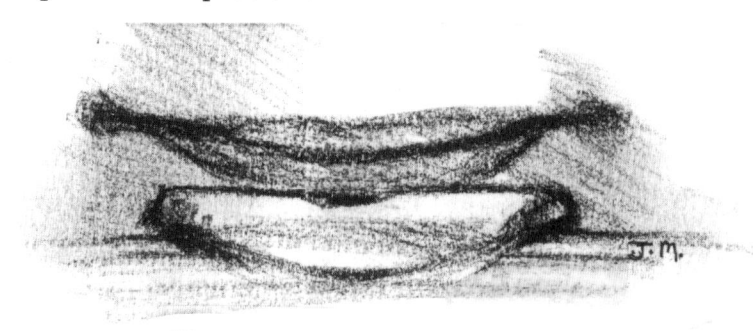

Octave leaps

Smiley embouchure   Incorrect

Dynamics & Tuning 55

As you pull the top lip down and make the air travel faster for the higher note, make sure you keep the top lip **well forward,** considerably further than the bottom lip, **at all times, for every note!**

Top lip forward

There are two very important reasons for keeping the top lip well forward at all times, but particularly so for the upper registers:

1. To ensure that the way in which the air-jets strikes the blowing edge is maintained.
   The feeling should always be that you are really blowing slightly more **into** the flute than across it. Experiments with altering the angle of the air-jet by, for instance, rolling the flute in or out as you blow can demonstrate that the most positive sound comes when you are blowing rather more down than across (of course blowing too much into the flute leads to poor sound quality). Because the jaw and (to some extent) the bottom lip must also be brought slightly further forward (for reasons explained below), the top lip must be progressively pulled **even further** forward to maintain the correct angle of air-jet. The top lip directs the air-jet in exactly the right way towards the blowing edge, like a spout or funnel. As the higher notes are reached and the jaw and bottom lip advance, the top lip extends forward almost to its furthest limit. This is particularly true when you are playing very softly on the high notes.

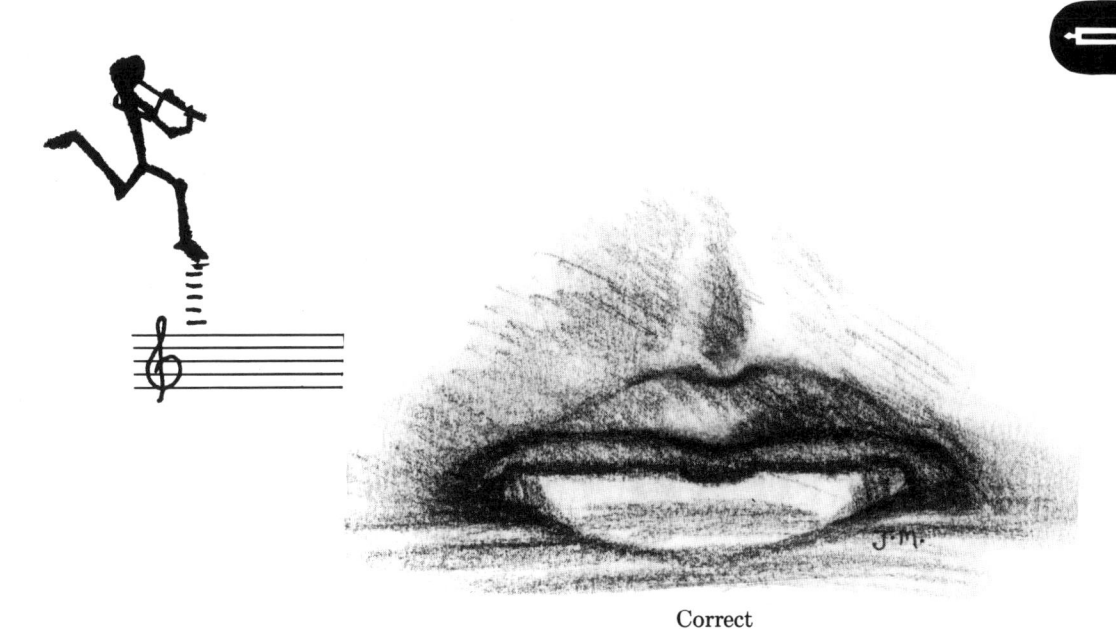

Correct

top lip more forward than bottom lip

Correct

straight bottom lip, top lip forward

Illustrated Fluteplaying

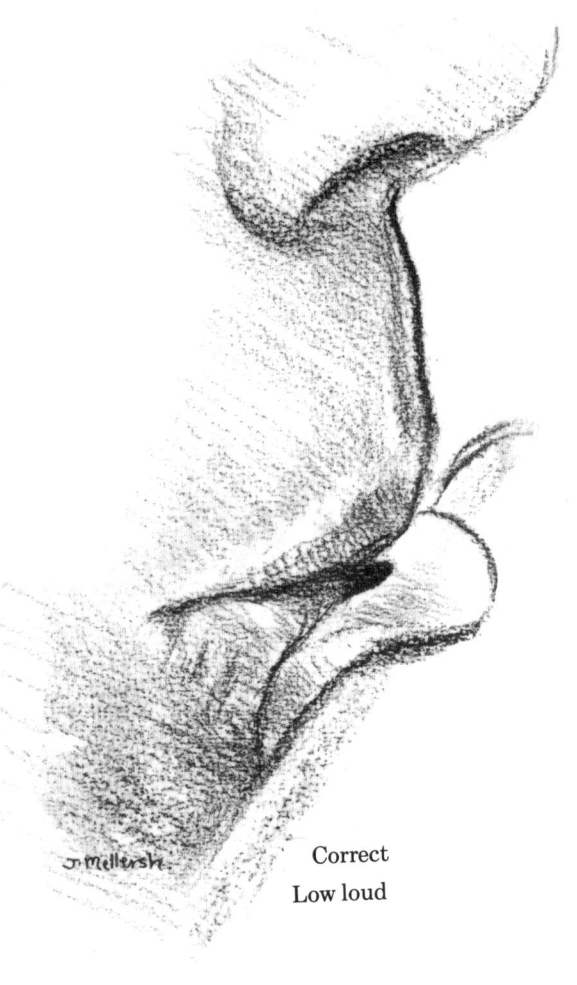

2. The top lip must also be kept well forward to maintain the correct-shaped aperture between the lips. If the top lip and bottom lip are **parallel** to each other (see page 67), the aperture will tend to be **slit-shaped** and "two-dimensional", without enough depth to let the air-jet emerge in precisely the correct way. When the top lip is pushed forward the aperture becomes more "three-dimensional", more like a funnel, which allows a stronger and more resonant sound to be produced, as this funnel-shape reinforces the resonance in the mouth cavity, which helps to produce a really singing sound, particularly in the high register (see page 15).

Cover hole with bottom lip

When you are playing a high note, created by a faster vibrating column of air inside the flute, it is almost like playing on a smaller instrument with a narrower bore, so the blow-hole ought, ideally, to be a fraction smaller in size to match. Because it is impossible to have a different-sized blow-hole for every note, the size of the hole is actually controlled by the amount of lower lip covering it, so for high notes you need to pout more over the hole with the fleshy red part of the middle of your lower lip, thus effectively reducing the size of the blow-hole. This adjustment is so **slight**, so **minute**, you can hardly see it, even close up to a mirror, but if you play, for example, a **low** G then a **top** G, the amount of lower lip movement might look like this:

Correct
Low loud

bottom G

The blow hole is covered less

top G

The blow hole is covered more

Again, because your bottom lip should be free to move in this way, try to keep it fleshy and fairly straight. A very smiley bottom lip stretches the critical fleshy red part in the middle and stops it from covering more or less of the blow-hole in an **even**, smooth movement.

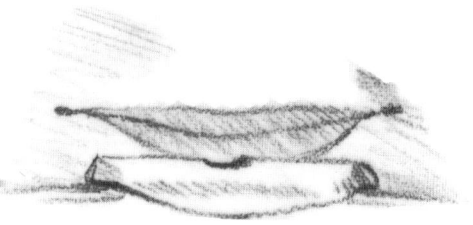

Too smiley   Incorrect

Incorrect

Too smiley

Dynamics & Tuning

Jaw movement

Finally, as you push the top lip forward and down, and pout slightly more over the hole, your **jaw** must move forward as well for the high note, otherwise the note tends to be flat. Although you adjust the top lip to keep a feeling of blowing more **into** the flute than across it, you must also slightly alter the **angle** at which the air-jet strikes the blowing wall, according to the pitch of the note. So high notes require a slightly less acute or downward angle compared to low notes: pushing the jaw forward achieves this adjustment, but remember to keep the flute absolutely still; don't roll it in or out even a millimetre, or the tone will suffer. The same effect of altering the angle of the air-jet comes from raising the head instead of moving the jaw forward, and some players use this method, finding jaw movements unnecessary; others use a combination of slight jaw and head movements. In the long run, each player can develop his own technique for controlling the angles at the blowing edge.

To sum up, jumping an octave involves: strongly controlled blowing from your abdominal muscles plus simultaneously moving:

— Top lip forward and down
— Bottom lip fractionally further over the hole
— Jaw forward slightly.

If you perform these movements evenly and to just the right degree, a high note should be effortless, easy to control, and in tune.

To prove how important all **three** movements are, try jumping or playing up through an octave while leaving one of the elements out:

a) Move jaw and lower lip, but don't move top lip — the upper note emerges breathy and unfocused.

b) Move top lip, but keep the jaw (or head) still — the upper note is thin and flat.

c) Don't move the lower lip further over the hole — the upper note sounds woolly and full of air.

So it's worth spending a lot of time playing up through octaves to get the feel of this smooth adjustment for the upper note always remembering that the **amount** of lip and jaw movement is extremely delicate and subtle; there are no jerky or violent movements involved. After a while the exact amount of adjustment becomes automatic as your ear and embouchure muscles work together to focus the note, and your breath pressure stays finely controlled at the right level.

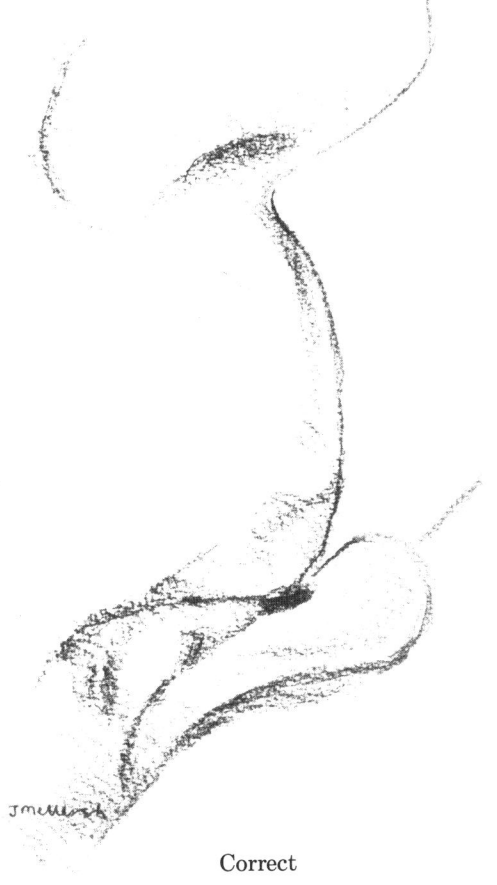

Correct
High loud

Octave leaps

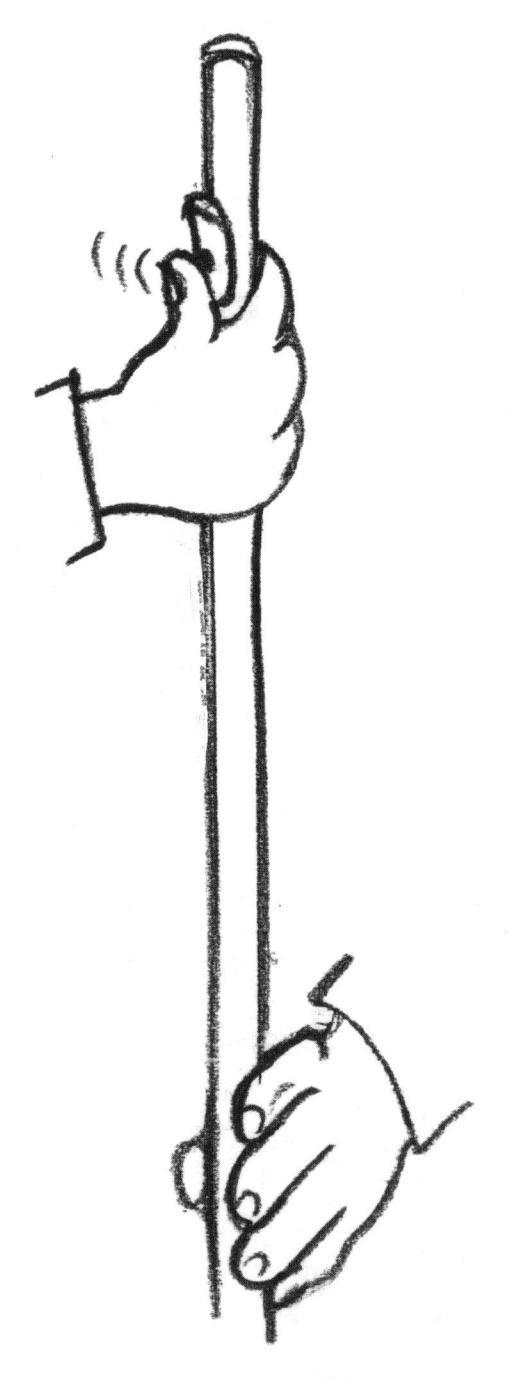

To change pitch accurately in smaller or larger intervals than an octave, exactly the same controls are used, but in smaller or larger degrees according to the interval. A major third, for example, requires such small adjustment that an observer does not notice any movement **at all,** whereas a leap of, say, two octaves, needs quite a noticeable change in the embouchure. A scale calls for a very gradual and smooth adjustment.

Jumping to lower notes from higher ones involve the reverse procedure to the one described above, so that:

— The lip-gap is **enlarged** by lifting the top lip, thus slowing the speed of the air-jet

— the lower lip covers slightly less of the blow-hole

— the jaw drops back a fraction.

This whole business of adjusting for changing pitch becomes totally effortless and automatic after a while, and no good player is consciously aware of making any movements, but we have tried to describe the details fully in order to help those who may not find things so easy at first.

Playing in tune

Try following these two experiments, which will help you to understand the way in which the pitch of a note is altered.

1. Take your flute and finger G (don't put it to your lips), tap down quite firmly; this gives you quite a good, hollow-sounding note. Now gradually move the ball of your right thumb over the blow-hole as you tap, and you hear the note getting flatter and flatter until it is almost an F sharp. (Covered completely it drops a 7th below G!)

This demonstrates that the amount of blow-hole covered by the bottom lip is crucial for basic tuning.

Dynamics & Tuning 59

2. Here is an exercise that may make this clearer. You can try **bending** a note by rolling the flute in and out (which in effect covers and uncovers more of the hole) as you blow, or by moving your head up and down (which has the same result). You should be able to alter the pitch of the note by at least a tone in this way, especially **below** the note.

Playing louder and softer in tune

If you play a note very softly and **simply blow harder** without moving your lips, jaw or head, the pitch of the note rises; it becomes sharp. Similarly, if you play a loud note and then blow more gently without adjusting, the note becomes very **flat**. So the strength of your breath pressure means that the angle of the air-jet must be directed **more** into the hole, while a less strong flow of air means that you must direct the air-jet more **across** the hole. To keep a note perfectly in tune as you vary the dynamics, you must alter the angle of the air-jet by subtle movements of your jaw:

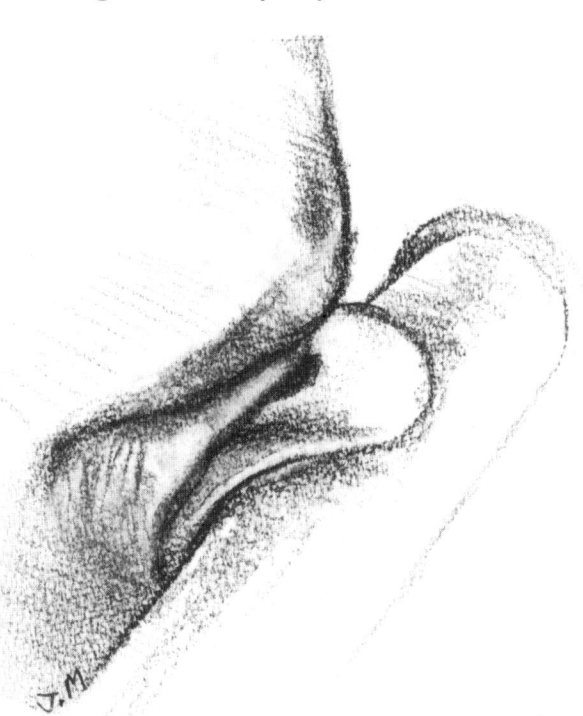

For soft playing keep jaw well forward, push top lip well forward.

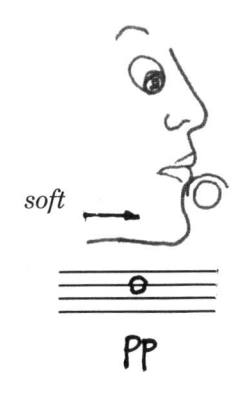

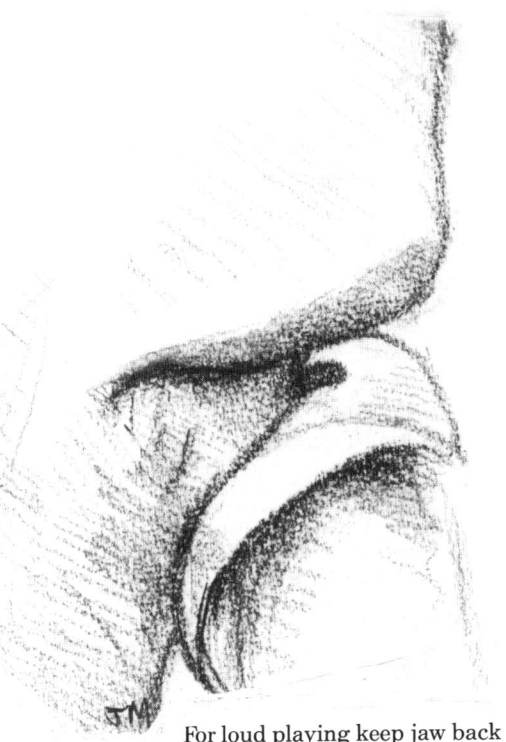

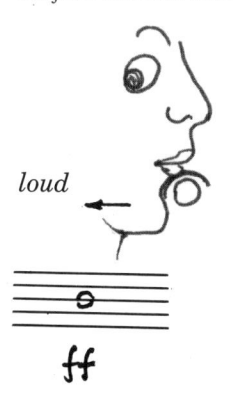

soft

pp

For loud playing keep jaw back pushing top lip down to direct the air-jet more into the flute.

loud

ff

Illustrated Fluteplaying

If you only move your jaw forward as you play softer, and nothing else, the tone quality of the note suffers — it becomes unfocused and rather breathy. So the **top lip** helps to funnel the air-jet in precisely the correct way against the blowing edge: as you get softer the top lip should move forward slightly, bringing the relatively slow-moving air-jet close up to the blowing edge.

The bottom lip stays in more or less the same position for the different dynamic levels of a note, but it is vital that the amount of hole covered for that note is correct; in other words, (as described on page 11), the bottom lip will be slightly further over the hole for a high note than it is for a low note.

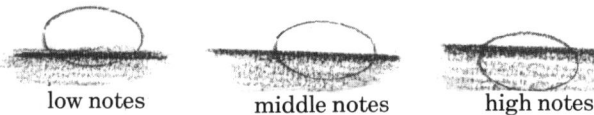

low notes   middle notes   high notes

Many people tend to play consistently flat because they have positioned the headpiece **too low on their lip**, with too much lip covering the hole. As explained by the first experiment above, this produces a flattening of pitch. Similarly, if the headpiece is rolled inwards too much, the same flattening results.

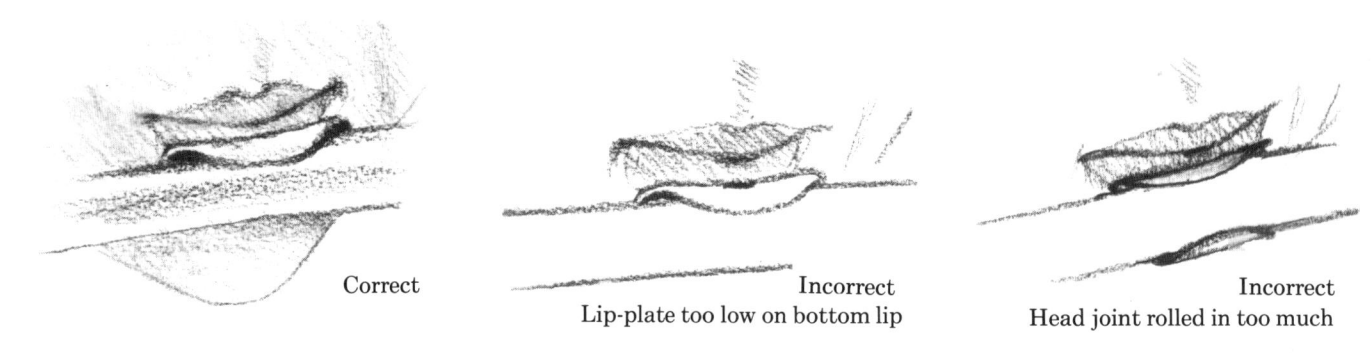

Correct   Incorrect — Lip-plate too low on bottom lip   Incorrect — Head joint rolled in too much

Other people may tend to play consistently sharp because they may have the headjoint **too high** on their lower lip, or rolled outwards too much.

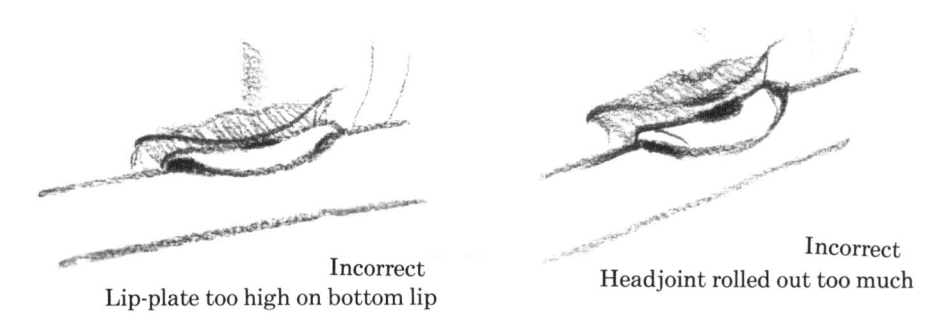

Incorrect — Lip-plate too high on bottom lip   Incorrect — Headjoint rolled out too much

So take trouble to find the best position of the
headjoint that suits **you** on your bottom lip, a position
that produces the most positive sound and which can
be played at the right pitch. Some people may need to
turn it in or out slightly to allow for their posture and
hand positions, others may keep the headjoint aligned
absolutely straight (as shown page 11). The main
thing is to keep the flute's position **still** on the lower
lip, and adjust the tuning mainly with the jaw plus
some top-lip movement.

To sum up

For soft playing:

Keep jaw forward, push top lip
well forward.

For loud playing:

Keep jaw back, push top lip **down**,
to direct the air-jet more into the flute.

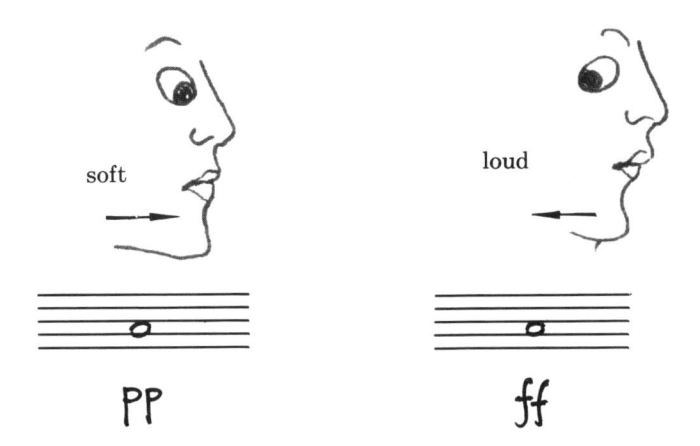

soft

loud

pp

ff

Don't expect your flute to "play in tune" for you!
There isn't such a thing as a perfectly "in-tune" flute.
Everything is ultimately the responsibility of the
player, so even if you have a flute that might have
some obviously sharp or flat notes in its make-up, it is
still possible to adjust the embouchure controls to
play exactly in tune every note!

Vibrato

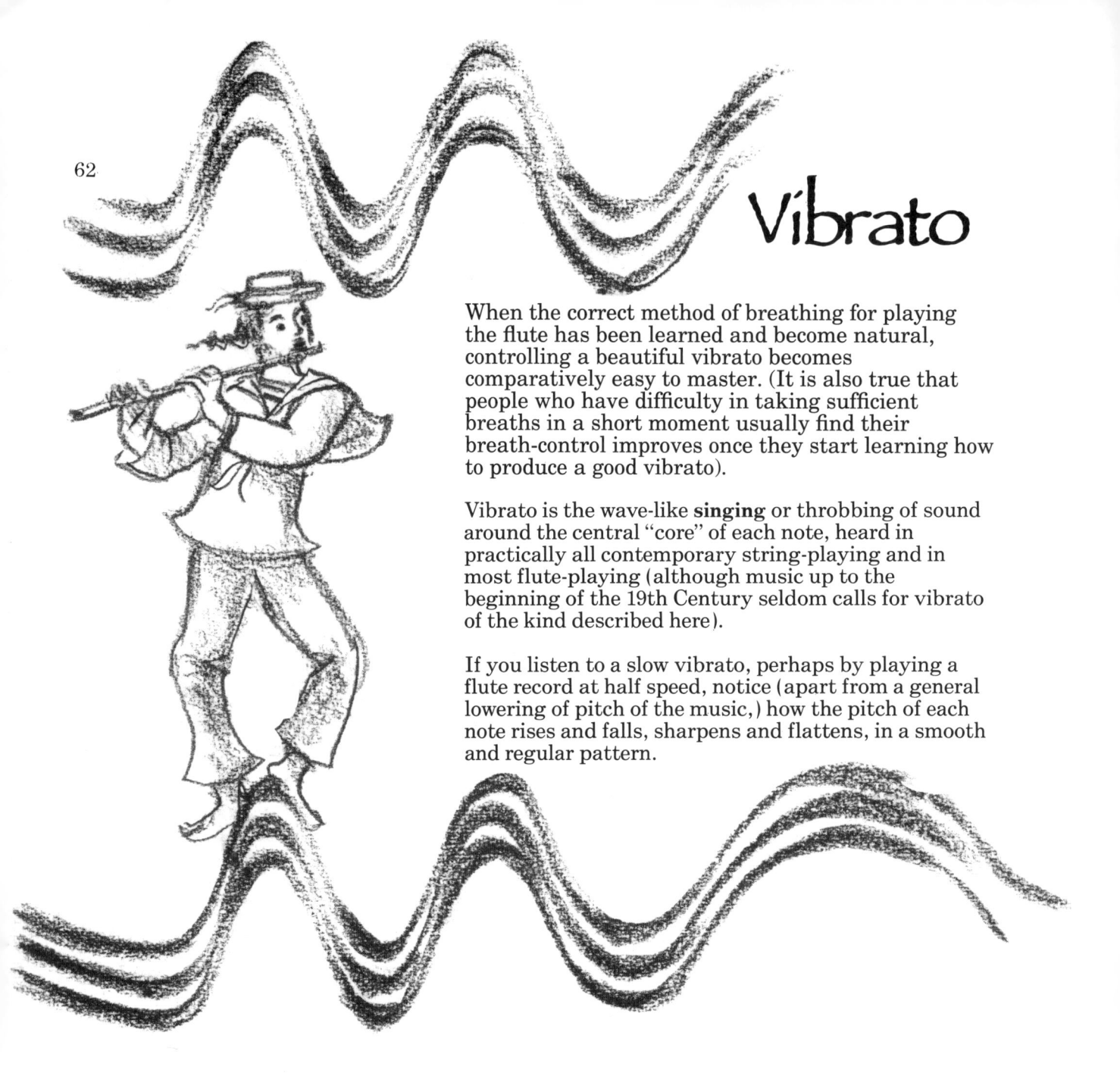

When the correct method of breathing for playing the flute has been learned and become natural, controlling a beautiful vibrato becomes comparatively easy to master. (It is also true that people who have difficulty in taking sufficient breaths in a short moment usually find their breath-control improves once they start learning how to produce a good vibrato).

Vibrato is the wave-like **singing** or throbbing of sound around the central "core" of each note, heard in practically all contemporary string-playing and in most flute-playing (although music up to the beginning of the 19th Century seldom calls for vibrato of the kind described here).

If you listen to a slow vibrato, perhaps by playing a flute record at half speed, notice (apart from a general lowering of pitch of the music,) how the pitch of each note rises and falls, sharpens and flattens, in a smooth and regular pattern.

A violinist gets this vibrato by, in effect, shortening and lengthening the string with his fingers to obtain a rapidly alternating series of sharper and flatter pitches round the basic note.

A flute-player raises and lowers the pitch for vibrato by simply blowing alternately more intensely and less intensely (harder and softer), **without** any adjustments for tuning. Assuming that the basic tone is well-focused and exactly in tune ("the middle of the note" is good), this pulsation causes the note to come alive and vibrate around its centre. Remember that nearly all the vibrato is a variation of **pitch**, and only a small proportion is a variation of **volume.** If you think of vibrato as merely blowing louder and softer the result will probably be uneven and ugly.

Vibrato

Once again, the fluctuating air-pressure required for vibrato is primarily controlled from the diaphragm and lower abdominal area, but a complicated series of muscles around the wind-pipe, throat, and larynx also play their part, and the cheeks are often used to help in the final effect by vibrating "in sympathy", and increasing the resonance of the note. Players vary in the exact way they use these muscles, but generally speaking most people's main vibrato control comes from the abdomen and diaphragm and not from the throat area. It is important to keep the throat **open** and fairly relaxed, as any tension is reflected in the sound: an uneven "bleating" effect is the result of tightening the throat or larnyx. Make sure you don't let your lips or jaw wobble for vibrato (although these techniques were often used by players in the past). For the same reason, the vibrato cannot be evenly controlled in this way.

Keep your throat OPEN

Air in cheeks vibrating in sympathy — remember the hamster.

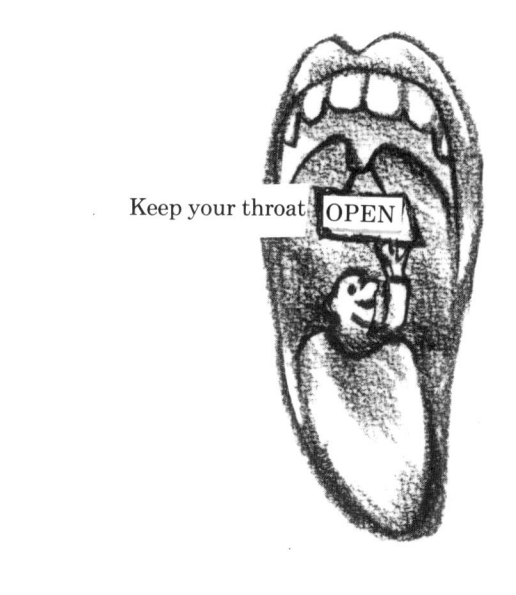

Learning Vibrato

The first step is to make sure that you play a note **without the slightest wobble at all**; if the note wavers or bleats, even a tiny bit, you must practise getting rid of the waver, or it will be difficult to control "proper" vibrato. It helps to use the mouthpiece of a treble or tenor recorder and practise blowing an even note on it: the wavers show up immediately because of the comparatively free flow of air that is needed to produce the sound.

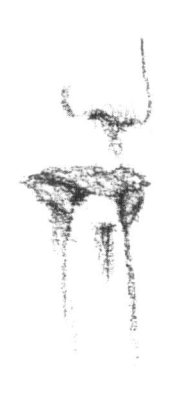

64 *Illustrated Fluteplaying*

When you can blow an even straight note on the recorder and the flute, learn how to produce some slow, even waves of air:

Without the flute, take a good deep breath and slowly exhale 5 or 6 sighs in the same breath, as in whispering "hoohh, hoohh, hoohh, hoohh, hoohh", until you think your lungs are empty. This should force you to bring your belly right in and up, and all the abdominal muscles should help to squeeze the last gasps out. If you can still whisper "hoola-hoop" you still have some air left, so practise pushing **all** the air out, putting your hands on your abdomen to feel the muscles relaxing.

Slowly exhale five or six sighs in the same breath.

Now, with the flute, blow 5 or 6 slow "hoohh's" on a low G, with small gaps between each "hoohh", but without taking in any air. Don't try to make a big sound as this may cause tensions round your throat or mouth and interfere with the smooth waves.
Next, join the "Hoohh's" together, trying to get an obvious flattening of pitch in the weak links between each "Hoohh":

Join the 'hoohh's' together

Aim for a very even, very slow wave pattern. Do this exercise in one breath and feel the diaphragm working hard, pushing the last dregs of air out. Listen for an equal rise and fall in pitch round the note: if you can hear this, then you are producing vibrato correctly.

When you can do this slow vibrato easily on one note, practise doing it on each note of a scale. First play the scale in semibreves, with **no** vibrato, checking that the notes are in tune and free from any tremor at all.

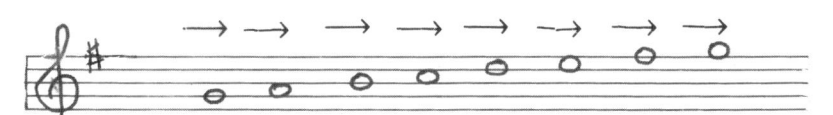

Now blow 4 slow waves on each note of the scale, taking a good breath between each note: keep it slow, keep it even, don't tense your throat or arms or lips, but play with a fairly weak and breathy sound for relaxation in all areas.

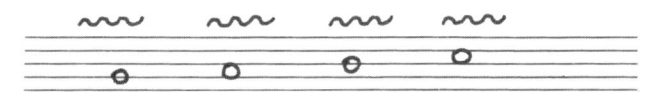

Be very careful not to increase the speed too rapidly, as throat vibrato may creep in and become superimposed on the regular waves, giving the "nanny-goat" effect.

Once this has been mastered, gradually increase the speed of the waves so that you can count 8 waves on each note, then 16, 32, 64, and so on.

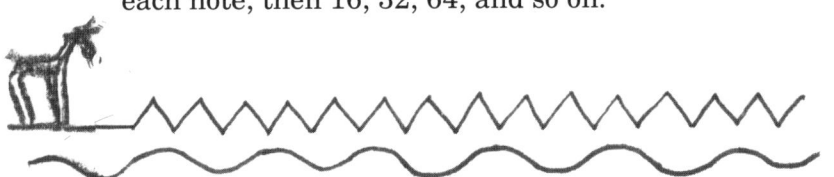

Throat vibrato gives the nanny-goat effect

Aim to vary the speed and intensity of the vibrato, both according to the expressive demands of the music, and between registers. As a rough rule, higher notes call for a faster vibrato than low ones, and pieces with slow tempo and sustained low-register playing are usually more effective with a fairly slow vibrato. It is useful to practise counting the vibrato on a scale, at first playing all the way up with the **same** vibrato; the next time increasing the speed of the vibrato as you ascend.

The eventual idea is to make the vibrato a totally inseparable part of the flute sound, not something added to it; vibrato should always be thought about with great care and used with discretion. There is no rule about when to use it and when not; it is very much up to the individual performer, but the main thing is to be in command of it at all times.

Blowing Problems

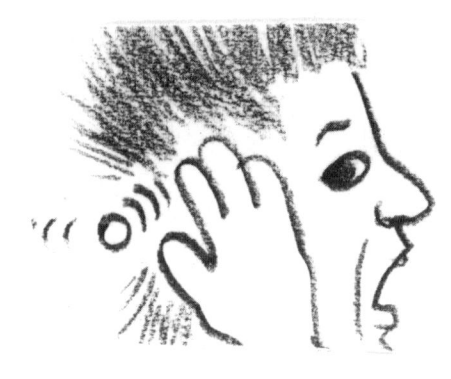

You can improve your sound when you have found the cause of your problem.

Tone Problems

Almost all tone problems are connected in some way to faults in breathing, embouchure control, or posture, and only a few are caused entirely by some anatomical or physical irregularity in the muscles round the mouth, in the lips, teeth, or jaw. It is nearly always possible to improve one's sound, if the cause of the problem has been identified.

Listed below are some of the commonest "tone problems" with their possible causes. The remedy to each problem is to eliminate each cause, one-by-one or in various combinations, until the sound improves. Very often, of course, an unsatisfactory sound may be linked to more than one symptom or cause, but we have tried to simplify the categories below.

1. Thin "strangled" sound

This sounds a bit like a magnified mosquito, with no depth or roundness.

Possible causes:

a) Headjoint rolled in too much

The air-jet is forced too low, and the high notes in particular are thin and lifeless.

b) Flute too low on bottom lip

Too much bottom lip covers the hole, and the sound is dulled and very flat.

Sounds like a magnified mosquito

Blowing Problems 67

c) Head is held down too much

This again causes the blow-hole to be covered too much.

d) Parallel lips

The top and bottom lips are parallel to each other, instead of the top lip coming forward. This makes for the wrong-shaped lip-aperture and an incorrect direction of the air-jet (as described on page 15).

Incorrect

Parallel lips

Incorrect

Too tight an embouchure

e) Too tight an embouchure

A tight smile or too much pressure from the top lip may prevent the air-jet from being sufficiently large to make the note respond correctly.

f) Tight throat

Either too much tension in the throat, causing it to close somewhat, or a wrong head or neck angle that constricts the air supply.

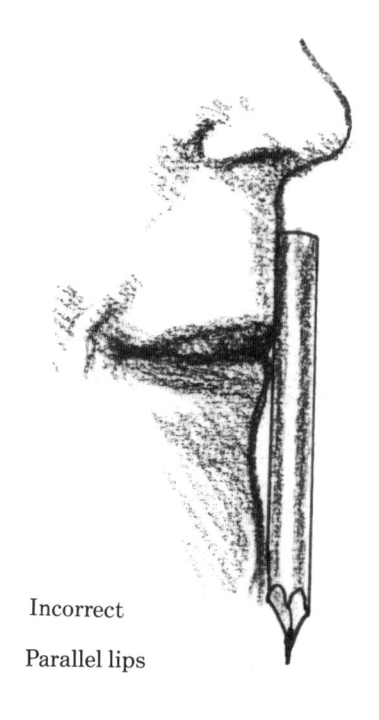

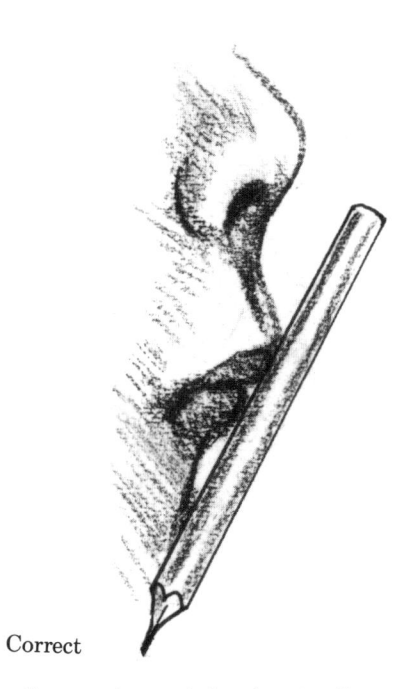

Correct

Top lip more forward than bottom lip

2. Woolly, husky, unfocused sound

There is no "middle" to the note, and half of the sound seems to be air-noise.
Possible causes

a) Headjoint rolled out too much

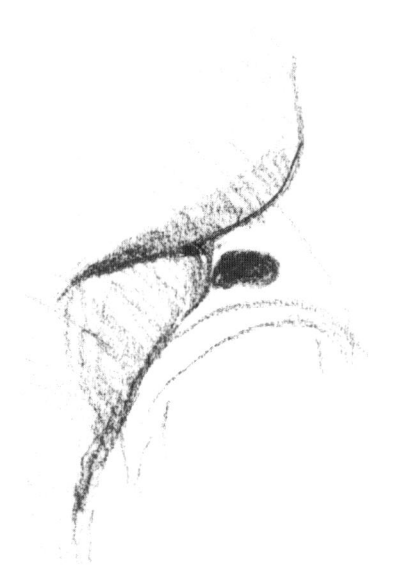

Not enough bottom lip covers the hole, with an inevitably breathy result. The top lip cannot direct the air-jet towards the blowing edge at the correct angle.

b) Flute too high on bottom lip

Again, not enough bottom lip covers the hole (same result as in 2a).

c) Head is held up too much

The same problem results as in 2a) and 2b).

d) Too large a lip-gap

The embouchure is so relaxed that the air-jet is too wide and it spills out incorrectly. The top lip may not be pushing down enough, or the corners of the bottom lip may be so floppy that there is lack of control at the centre.

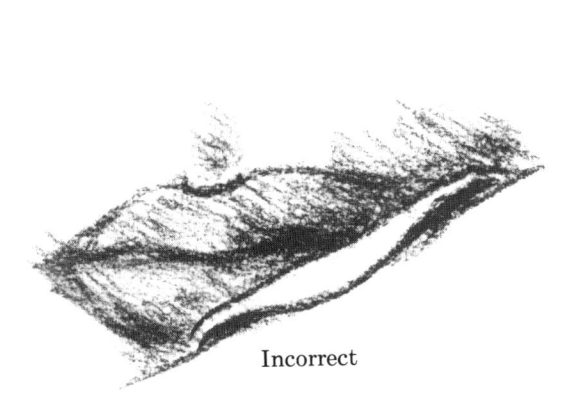

Incorrect

Correct

The air-jet strikes the blowing edge at the wrong angle in a horizontal sense (rather than in a vertical sense), so that there is spillage and wasted air.

f) Faults in posture such as stooping, slouching, resting the flute on the left shoulder, keeping it too near the right shoulder, and so on, will prevent the angles from being precisely aligned, and the resulting sound is unfocused.

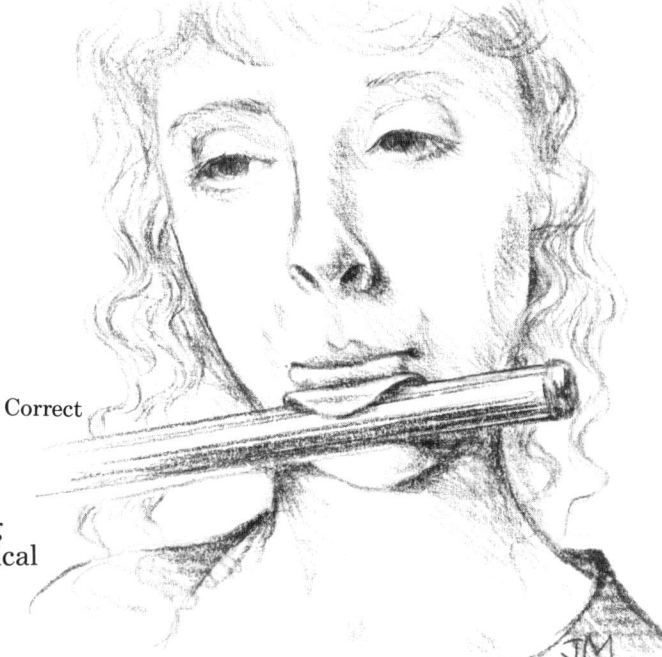

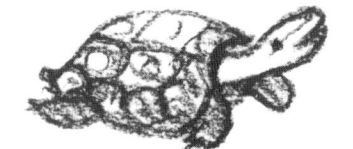

Remember the tortoise

3. Weak low notes

Possible causes

a) Weak top lip

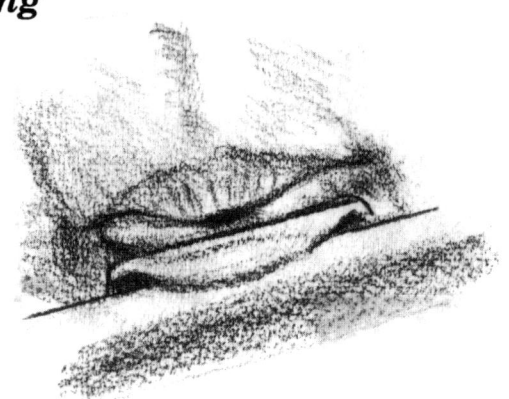

The centre of the top lip doesn't "clamp down" onto the air-jet sufficiently firmly, so that the lip-aperture is too wide for the note. Plenty of "rabbit" exercises should help to strengthen the top-lip movement.

b) Bottom lip uncontrolled

As in 2d) the lack of any sideways tension in the bottom lip allows too large a lip-gap to be formed.

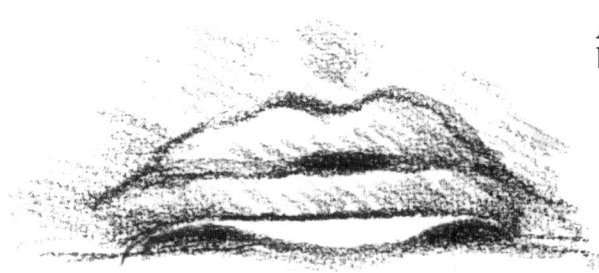

c) Jaw pulled back too far

The air-jet is directed downwards too much, into the hole causing dull and feeble low notes.

d) Head held down too much

A common habit is putting the head "low" to play low notes, as this might seem the natural way to play them, but the result is once again an air-jet that enters the blow-hole too far in.

4. *Forced or split high notes*

The top notes are thin and piercing, with a feeling of insecurity in the sound.

Possible causes

a) Rigid embouchure (or "Frozen Chops")

The embouchure is basically tight and inflexible, preventing the subtle movements of "the three controls": everything is "frozen", so that the lips and jaw are fixed in a position which might produce good middle-register notes but will not give the upper notes any chance of sounding controlled and rounded. This rigid embouchure is often accompanied by tightness in the throat and cheeks, cutting down any helpful resonance to the sound.

b) "Elbow waggling"

Don't get carried away!

Incorrect

It seems natural to some to lift the left elbow as they play from low notes to upper ones, but of course this tends to roll the flute inwards, causing the sound to become thin and very flat.

All these four categories (strangled sound, woolly sound, weak low notes, forced high notes) are, above all, influenced by good or bad **breathing** and diaphragm control. If the breathing is shallow and the abdomen and diaphragm are not working together, the sound is drastically affected, even if the embouchure is superb and the posture is perfect! Correct breathing is absolutely fundamental to getting a good sound.

Illustrated Fluteplaying

Poor Tone Quality caused by Physical or Anatomical Factors

1. Top lip problems

As already explained in this book, the central blob of the top lip (the tubercle) is crucial in its action as the leading edge of the "valve" effect of the top lip, but in some people this part of their anatomy is missing.

e.g.   a)

"The Bermudan Triangle"

Small area at centre of top lip missing

b) and the Hare Lip

Remedy

It is often possible to overcome these problems to some extent by regular use of top lip exercises: the top lip and the scowling muscles become so strong that it's possible to **flatten** the lip membrane at the centre.

Lip press-ups

ABh missing triangle doesn't really affect the sound too much until you reach the upper registers, and then it makes it especially difficult to get a good clear sound. To overcome this, try lip-press-ups, rabbit exercises, and practise of arpeggios, concentrating on pushing the top lip well forward and down, as well as **lipping** notes, and by playing a tune or scale without the tongue, but pushing the top lip down to start each note.

Lip trainer

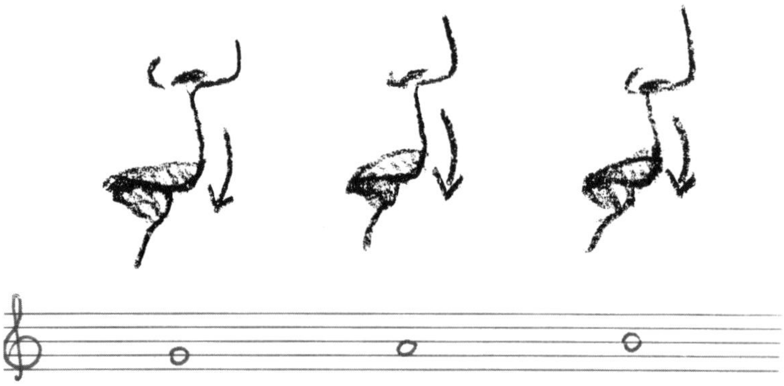

etc to high register

Blowing Problems 73

c) The two-holer

Here the well developed central tubercle cuts the lip-gap in two. The sound is usually unfocused, or even split, and top notes are extremely difficult to control.

Two possible remedies

Either: try to develop a central hole. Take a fine drinking straw and form an embouchure round it, or sharpen a typist's hard eraser to form a point and use this in the same way.

Or: learn to blow from **one** of the two holes, closing the other. You need to get close in front of a mirror and play on the headjoint alone at first: after much patient work it is possible to control this embouchure quite effectively.

Two-holer

Blowing from the side

Rabbit exercise

d) The short top lip

The difficulty here is getting the top lip far enough forward and down to be able to control the air-jet in the correct way. However, lip-press-ups, rabbit, and similar exercises, will again help to develop the top-lip muscles, and it is possible to change the shape of the embouchure quite dramatically. It is also useful to practise stretching the top lip onto the far side of the lip-plate.

Whistling a note without the flute, and then blowing a note with the same feeling of a forward whistling pout may help get the top lip to stretch a bit more.

Lip press-ups

74   *Illustrated Fluteplaying*

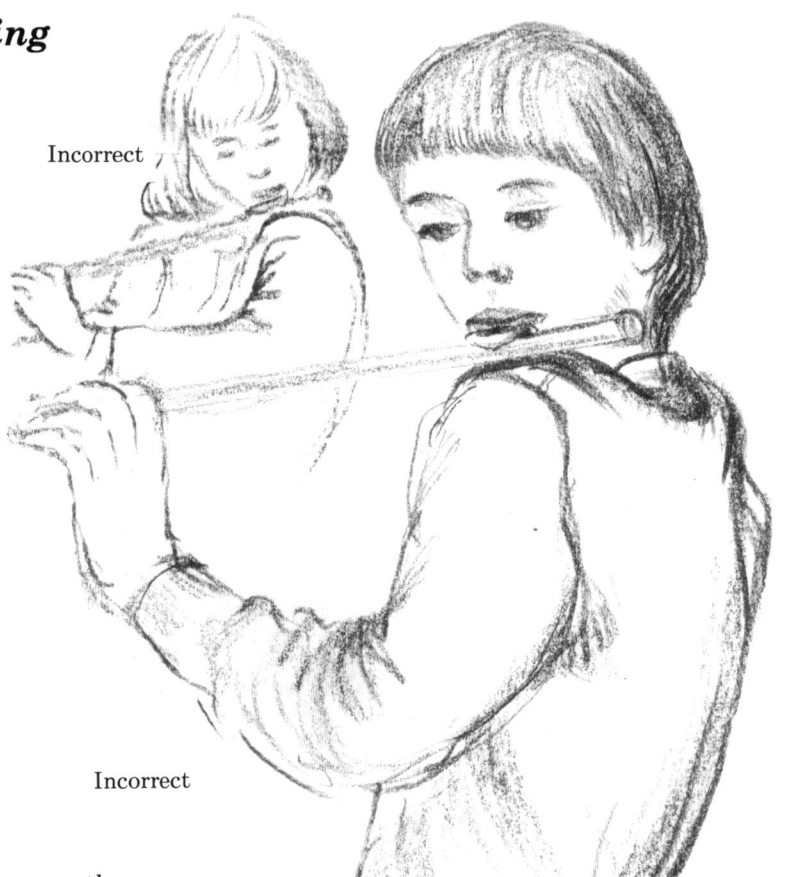

Incorrect

Incorrect

2. Blowing from the side

Some people develop a side embouchure because they started the flute at an early age (perhaps 7 or 8), when it was difficult to reach the keys, and the flute seemed so heavy that they rested it on the left shoulder:

This position forces the angle of lips and flute out of alignment, and the muscles round the embouchure adjust accordingly. The recent introduction of curved-head flutes is intended to overcome this difficulty:

Correct

Curved head helps overcome difficulties

Incorrect

Too small to manage a standard flute

Blowing Problems

A tall junior
Incorrect

If a child is rather tall for his age he may stoop and crane his neck forward, pulling the flute to the right, and creating a lip-gap to the left of the embouchure: the "Tall Junior" (see page 23).

Other early habits, like slouching, keeping the elbows too far in, holding the flute too low, or standing badly, all tend to produce an off-centre embouchure.

A cross-legged sloucher
Incorrect

Elbows too close to body
Incorrect

It is quite possible to play very successfully with a side embouchure (many professional players do), but the fact that there is an **imbalance** in the embouchure muscles can sometimes affect tone production quite seriously, particularly in the upper register where things are so critical.

Occasionally the centre of the lips may be insensitive or slightly roughened (for instance, excessive tea or coffee drinking, smoking, and alcohol all tend to produce an area of less sensitive membrane at the centre of the lips), and a side embouchure may therefore be more precisely controllable.

Blowing from the side
Not Recommended

3. Teeth

There are not usually any blowing problems associated with the type of teeth you have, but excessively protruding top teeth may prevent the top lip from coming down properly:

It is quite possible to play successfully with dentures or a brace — a sympathetic dentist can help ensure that you can still keep some pressure on your jaw and lower lip, and bring your top lip forward and down, without looseness or interference from your unfamiliar dental paraphernalia!

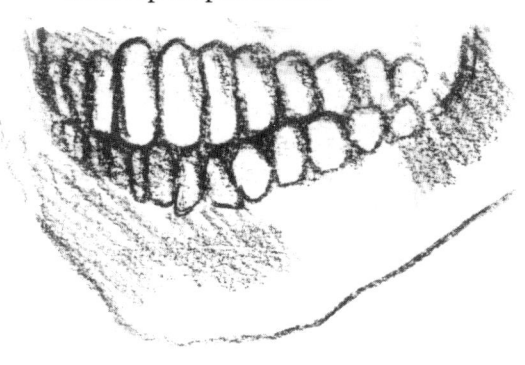

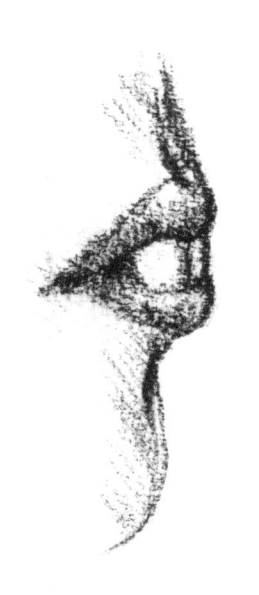

76 *Illustrated Fluteplaying*

Conclusion

We hope that you have found this book a useful companion to your flute playing, helping to give you a firm foundation for a good technique and an expressive sound — a sound that is uniquely **your** sound. All the hard work involved in regular and concentrated practise of tone exercises, scales, studies and so on will pay off in the end, provided you are fully aware of **how** and **why** the breathing, posture, fingers, vibrato etc. must be in complete control. This book is both an introduction to these matters, and a guide which can be used for reference even at quite an advanced stage: fluteplayers are always aiming to improve their sound, which is one of the most enjoyable (and often frustrating!) challenges of learning the instrument.

Index

abdomen, twisting 52
abdominal breathing 49
abdominal muscle control 63, 64, 71, 45, 47
aching
   muscles 24
   neck 21, 33
   shoulder 18
air jet
   size 6, 7
   strength 59
   speed of 15, 54, 55, 58, 60
   angle 66, 69
   angle and tuning 57
   control 36-39, 73
   experiments 5
   shaping 56
   under pressure 54
air noise 68
air, passing down windpipe 47
altering pitch 59
anatomical reasons for poor tone 72
angles for playing
   body angles 18
   chair and stand angles, when sitting 24
   elbow angle 35
   flute and body angle 18
   flute and lip angle 19
   flute to mouth angle 35
   head angle 18, 67
   trunk angle 24
   under arm angle 33
   wrist and arm angle 31
angle of air jet 59, 67, 69, 70
arm hooker 25
arms 25, 34, 35
arpeggio exercises 72
assembly of flute 2, 3

back 24, 25
back away from chair 52
banana fingers 33
bending the note 59
Bermudan triangle 72
bicycle pump plunger 50
bleating vibrato 63, 65
blowhole central 73
blowhole coverage 11, 48, 56, 58, 59, 66, 67, 68

blowhole, turning in or out 60, 68
blowing
   blowing problems 23, 33, 66-75
   control 18
   down too much 23
   introduction 6
   harder 54
   intensely 62
   too hard 42
   correct 43
bottom lip 5-8
   blowhole coverage 58, 68
   control 70
   flute still on 61
   movement 56
   parallel with top 56
   same for loud and soft 60
   straight 54
breadbin exercise 8
breath control 57, 59, 62
breath, running out of 42
breathing 20, 42-53, 53, 62
   problems 18, 23
   constricted 25, 33
   control 18, 30
   correct 22
   freely 24
   exercises 53
   in 44, 46-48, 50
      against pressure 53
      through mouth 46
      inefficiently 48
      mechanism 49
      muscles 43
      automatic pilot 43
   out 44, 49
      properly 42
      quality 71
      tone 60
      with diaphragm 45
breathy sound 54, 68

cavities in throat, nose, mouth 51
chair, position on 21, 24-25
changing pitch and dynamics 54
cheek vibration for resonance 63
cheeks tight 71
chest muscles 45, 47, 48

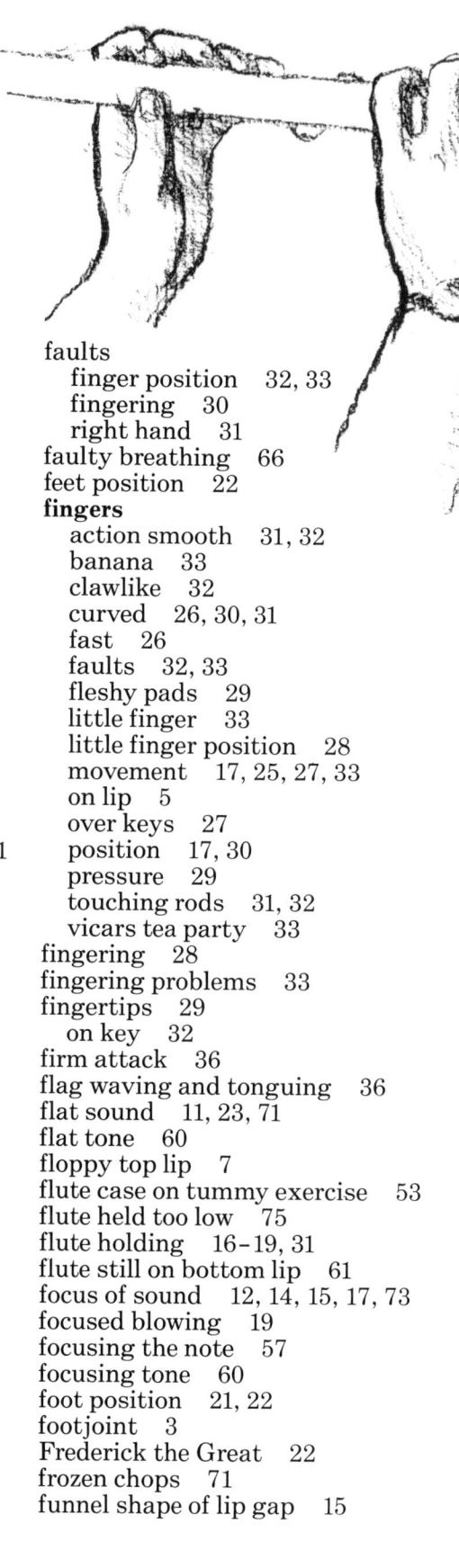

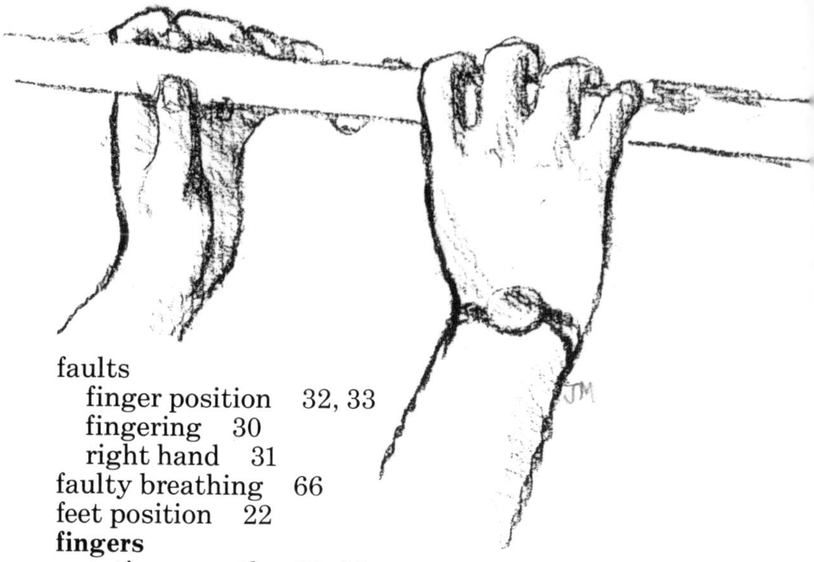

Illustrated Fluteplaying

cleaning flute   2, 4
concertina like rib-cage   47
cork position   4
corners of mouth   69
coverage of blow hole etc   11
craning neck   23, 75
crossed legs   23, 25, 52
crown   4
curved head joints   74

depressing keys   29
diaphragm   44, 45
  as fine tuning device   49
  control   71
  descends   46
  muscle control   63, 64
difficulty in reaching keys   30
drooping fingers   33
dynamics and jaw position
dynamics and tuning   54, 55, 56, 57, 58, 59, 60, 61
elbow height   34, 35, 75
elbow waggling   34, 71
elbows   33, 34, 35
embouchure   5
  adjustments   61
  adjustments between different notes   12
  and tonguing   38
  balance of muscles   19
  control   5, 66, 73
  for high notes   57
  muscles   18 42, 74
  off centre   75
  rigid   71
  resistance at   49
  smiling   54
exercise jaw back and forward   10
exercise bending the note   59
exercise breathing   50, 53
exercise for tuning   59
experiments on pitch   58

faults
  finger position   32, 33
  fingering   30
  right hand   31
faulty breathing   66
feet position   22
fingers
  action smooth   31, 32
  banana   33
  clawlike   32
  curved   26, 30, 31
  fast   26
  faults   32, 33
  fleshy pads   29
  little finger   33
  little finger position   28
  movement   17, 25, 27, 33
  on lip   5
  over keys   27
  position   17, 30
  pressure   29
  touching rods   31, 32
  vicars tea party   33
fingering   28
fingering problems   33
fingertips   29
  on key   32
firm attack   36
flag waving and tonguing   36
flat sound   11, 23, 71
flat tone   60
floppy top lip   7
flute case on tummy exercise   53
flute held too low   75
flute holding   16-19, 31
flute still on bottom lip   61
focus of sound   12, 14, 15, 17, 73
focused blowing   19
focusing the note   57
focusing tone   60
foot position   21, 22
footjoint   3
Frederick the Great   22
frozen chops   71
funnel shape of lip gap   15

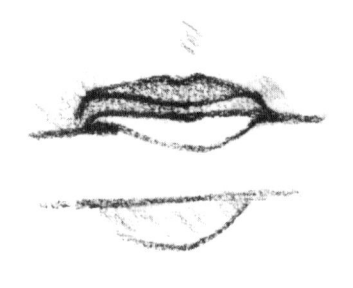

Index

garden hose 54
gauge for cork position 4
grease 4
group playing 21
hand positions 26-33
hare lip 72
head
  angle of 18
  craning forward 33
  drooping 25
  turned 20
  and neck angle 67
  and neck positions 51
  position 67, 70
headjoint 2-8, 10-12
  curved 74
headjoint rolled in 66
height of flute on lip 66, 68
high note
  control 71, 73
  vibrato 65
  and Bermudan triangle 72
  and off centre embouchure 75
  thin and piercing 71
  embouchure for 57
holding
  angles 19
  away from right shoulder 20
  body when assembling 2
  correct angle 22
  position 24
horse face 9
hose, and breathing 49
hunched shoulders 23

index finger 16
intonation
  introduction 1
  control **30**
  problems 25

jaw 10, 16-17, 57-60
  and bottom lip forward 55
  movement and air jet angle 57
  movement and tuning 57, 59
  position 70
jerky key pressing 27
jumping from high to low notes 58
jumping into freezing lake 50
jumping octaves 54, 57

key
  action 29
  noises 29
  pressing 27
King Frederick the Great 22

lining up flute and face 19
lining up headjoint 2
lip
  exercises 9
  muscle change between notes 12
  press-ups 7, 72, 73
  and jaw wobble 63
  lip gap control 7, 19
  lip gap size 14, 15, 56, 58, 69, 70
  parallel 67
lip-plate 2, 4, 10
lipping notes 72, 73
little finger 28, 31, 33
loud playing 42, 59, 61
low notes
  on headjoint 12
  problems 31
  control 70, 71
  vibrato 65
  feeble 70, 71
lung capacity 43
lungs deflate 49
lungs inflate 47, 50

military posture 48
mirror work 5, 9, 19
moisture on pads 4
morse code 36
mosquito buzz 66
mouth, breathing in through 46
muscles
  abdominal muscles, supportive not hard 45
  back 52
  between ribs 45
  breathing 43
  chest muscles 45
  mouth 45
  support in breathing 50
  tummy and chest 45
  cramped 31
  of body 18
music stand 20, 24

nanny goat vibrato   65
neck   21, 23, 33
neck and head positions   51
nostrils stretched down   9
notch on cleaning rod   4

oboe reed   42
octave leap   54
off centre blowing   19
off centre embouchure   74, 75
open holes   29
open throat   63
orchestral playing   21

palms of hands   26, 27
panting after running   43
parallel lips   56, 67
parrot fingers   32
pin prick shock   50
pitch
   sharp and flat   60
   adjusting for   58
   control   58
   variation   62
playing in tune   54, 58, 59, 61
playing louder or softer   59
polishing flute   4
poor tone, anatomical reasons for   72
position
   chair   21
   foot joint   3
   hand   26
   head and arms   20
   lip plate on bottom lip   8
   music stand   21
   sitting   19
   standing   19
position of flute on bottom lip   60, 61
posture   20, 22, 71
   and blowing problems   66
   for breathing   47
   problems   74
   sitting   52
pout movement over hole   57
pouting   6
pressure
   of fingers   29
   of lip on jaw   1
pressure of airflow   49
pressure points   16, 31
   index finger lowest joint   28
problems
   low note problems   31
   right arm   25

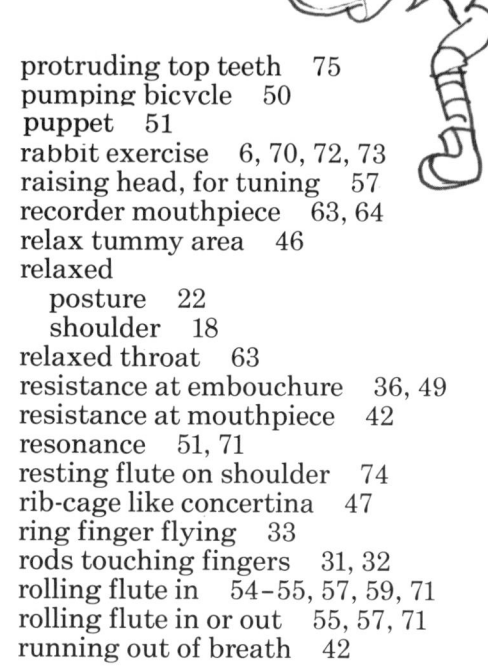

protruding top teeth   75
pumping bicycle   50
puppet   51
rabbit exercise   6, 70, 72, 73
raising head, for tuning   57
recorder mouthpiece   63, 64
relax tummy area   46
relaxed
   posture   22
   shoulder   18
relaxed throat   63
resistance at embouchure   36, 49
resistance at mouthpiece   42
resonance   51, 71
resting flute on shoulder   74
rib-cage like concertina   47
ring finger flying   33
rods touching fingers   31, 32
rolling flute in   54-55, 57, 59, 71
rolling flute in or out   55, 57, 71
running out of breath   42

saliva interference and tonguing   38
shape of lip gap   15
sharp sound   11, 54
sharp tone   60
short top lip   7, 73
shoulder position for breathing   47
shoulders   18, 21, 34
sideways embouchure   19, 73, 75
sideways tension in bottomlip   70
silent breathing   50
singing resonance   51
sitting   19-21, 24-25
size of lip gap   49, 69
sliding finger in and out of headjoint   12
slit shape of lip gap   15, 56
slouching   52, 75
slow vibrato   64
slow vibrato study   62
smiley embouchure   9, 54, 67
smiling bottom lip problems   56
smooth finger movements   32
soft playing   42, 61, 59
soldier posture   48
sound
   control of   16
   making the best   14, 15
speed of air jet   54, 55, 58
standing   19, 22, 23, 52
start of note   37
starting to blow   5, 11

stifled sound 11
stooping 23, 75
straight
  back 24
  wrists **30**
straight bottom lip 54, 56
strain
  avoiding 19
  neck muscle 21
strangled sound 71
strength of top lip 70
stretch lip corners 9
stronger sound 56
support from muscles 50

tall children 23, 75
tapping a sound on flute 58
teeth 75
teeth and tongue 38
tension, avoiding 19
thin sound 51, 54, 66, 71
three controls 15, 54, 57, 58, 71
three pressure points 16
three stages of breathing 46
throat and larynx muscle control 63
throat
  constriction 51
  muscle tension 64
  open 63
  relaxed 63, 46
  tight 47, 67, 71
thumb
  as pressure point 16
  poker 32, 33
  position 27, 31
  sore thumb 17
  straight 30
tight embouchure 67
tight joints on flute 4
tight throat 63, 67
tight throat and cheeks 51
tilt of flute to face 19
tip of tongue movement 39
tone 20
  jaw position and 10
  control 18, 30, 35
  problems 66
  quality 60
tongue 36-39
tonguing 36-39
toothpaste tube and breathing 49
top lip 6, 9, 38
  air jet 57
  as main valve 54

Index 81

  exercises 72
  forward and down 55, 57, 72, 73
  forward for soft notes 60
  parallel with bottom 56
  pressures on air jet 54
  pressure 69
  problems 72
  pulled down 54
  sensitive 75
  strength 70
  stretching exercises 73
  well forward 56
tortoise 75
tortoise neck 23
trunk angle 20
tubercle of top lip 72
tummy and chest muscles 45
tummy expanding 43, 47
tummy movement 46, 53
tummy movement when tonguing 36
tuning
  by pulling out headjoint 2
  control of 35
  head moved up & down 59
  jaw position and 10
  with head 59
  problems 25, 33, 35
  and jaw movements 57
  with jaw and bottom lip 61
turbulence in flute 42
turning blowhole 60-61
twisting abdomen 52
twisting action 2
two-holer 73

unbalanced standing 23
uneven fingering 30
unfocused sound 42, 54

vibrating column of air 42, 56
vibrato 62, 63, 65
vicar's tea party 33
violin vibrato 62
volume variation 62

waggler, elbow 35, 71
washer in flute 4
weak low notes 70
weak sound 11, 42
weight distribution 22
windpipe 47
woolly sound 11, 37, 42, 71, 68
wrist 26-33

yawning when breathing in 46
young players 74